# Voices of חope

## 36 Essays Written in Response to 7 October

### Edited by Simon Eder and Adam Zagoria-Moffet

In collaboration with
**Louis Jacobs Foundation**
*louisjacobs.org*

*The transliteration schemes used by contributors for romanising Hebrew words are honoured as written and therefore vary throughout the course of this book.*

# Contents

# HEAL

# HOPE

הַדְרִיכֵנִי בַאֲמִתֶּךָ וְלַמְּדֵנִי
כִּי אַתָּה אֱלֹהֵי יִשְׁעִי
אוֹתְךָ קִוִּיתִי כָּל הַיּוֹם.

Guide me to Your truth and teach me,

for You, my God are my rescue –

it is upon You that I hope, all of the day.

Psalms 25.5 | תהילים כה:ה

# Introduction

We first heard of the terrible attacks in Israel, like so many others across the Jewish world within a few hours of those horrendous events on the 7th October. It was of course only days later that the extent of the tragedy began to emerge and even now, several weeks later, there are still some of the most shocking atrocities, that truly defy imagination, which are still coming out. This was the worst day to have befallen Israel in its 76 year history and indeed the worst day that the Jewish people have encountered since the Shoah.

It is of course too early to contextualise these events or perhaps to say anything truly meaningful about them. Indeed when inviting submissions for this compilation, the response of many was that the time was not right yet or that their grieving did not lend itself to words. There is a time for silence, which certainly must be respected. I think in the Torah of that episode from Leviticus when Aaron witnesses the death of his two sons, Nadav and Avihu and he is left devoid of speech. And yet perhaps the overwhelming Jewish response to destruction is with words - words that offer comfort, give strength and those that are grounded in the enduring values of Torah.

In fact, just as the prophets wrote during times of conflict and often grave difficulty for Israel presenting messages of renewal and addressing challenging political, social and religious situations, so too with some of today's leading thinkers, rabbis and theologians from across the Jewish spectrum, these short essays are designed to proffer hope. They too discuss the complexities that as a people both within Israel and far beyond its borders too, we face, in the shadow of these barbaric acts.

It has been difficult to categorise many of the entries as their themes certainly overlap. Some are very much in the form of convocations for those traumatised and who have been left bereft. Some reflect on the deep pain and anguish of war. There are those who urge caution as to the Israeli military's response and question whether real peace and security can ever be truly achieved through might. If there is one common thread throughout all the essays it is to the acknowledgement of the sanctity of all life. It is profoundly tragic to think that on the very day that Hamas wrought such havoc the Torah reading for the festival of Simchat Torah, from the opening of the Book of Genesis, reminds us that each human being is created in the image of God.

Whilst fitting the essays into neat delineation proved tricky, the subject matters under which the entries are arranged of 'HOME', 'HEAL' and 'HOPE' do seem most appropriate. On the 7th October, as women, babies and the elderly were brutally murdered in their own houses or taken hostage not on the front line but in the very neighbourhood in which they were raised, it is the very notion of these three concepts that was shattered. They must therefore warrant our reflection and reemphasis in the aftermath of these events.

# HOME

Anyone who has stepped foot in Israel has felt that feeling of home and today, certainly the destiny of the entire Jewish people is bound up with that of the land. To see within only a few generations the language of the Bible spoken again on its streets, to witness the thriving economy that Israel has become, that safeguards the rights of its citizens and maintains freedom of religion for all, is nothing short of miraculous and must at all costs be preserved.

It is not of course only the notion of 'HOME' in Israel itself that has been threatened by the violent acts but wherever Jews dwell. The last few weeks have seen a surge in antisemitism across the globe as Jewish day schools have cancelled classes, synagogues doors have been locked and social media has pulsated with hatred.

Frightening threats at Ivy League campuses in America have left Jews wondering whether their safety can be guaranteed in the US. In the UK, the Community Security Trust has said that the number of incidents in the three weeks following the attacks in Israel have been the highest of any period since data began to be collected more than thirty years ago. In France there have already been more than 400 arrests connected to antisemitic incidents in the weeks following the attacks. In Russia an angry crowd stormed an airport in the Dagestan region searching for Jews to harm after a plane arrived from Tel Aviv.

Nearly a century after the rise of Nazism, Jews are being threatened for who they are. To have a corner on earth therefore, that Jews can call home, within the geographical space that has borne Judaism's soul-print for millennia is pivotal for Jewish survival not only in Israel but everywhere.

# HEAL

Israel was quite possibly never as divided as it had been in the months and weeks leading up to the October savagery. The sweeping judicial reforms had triggered nationwide protests and much deep and anxious consideration between various camps as to the meaning of a Jewish democratic state. All this, which no doubt was part of the reason for authorities taking their eye off the security ball, has most unequivocally been put on ice as the nation has rallied together following the onslaught.

There has been nothing quite as moving as watching the emergence of Jewish unity unfold across Israel and the wider Jewish world too. It has manifested itself in the countless acts of *hesed* (loving kindness) following the attacks. We have seen it through the words of the poignant song, 'Coming Home' for those hostages, babies, mothers and the elderly amongst them, who remain in captivity. We have observed it in the Shabbat table installation that has now been erected in numerous locations across the world or the peaceful solidarity rallies to again raise awareness for the hostages. We have detected it through the way that families and communities have come together in tears and in song.

It is not, of course, only amongst Jews that healing is necessary following these attacks - it is also with the Palestinians, too. Indeed some of the essays urge, with almost prophetic warning, the emphatic need to reach out to 'The Other'. Many of the contributors are locked into the narrative of *realpolitik* which has thus far won out in terms of the possible Zionisms on offer since Israel's inception. There are however those whose sentiments direct us away from the "either us or them" calculus and to adopt in Martin Buber's phrase a "greater realism" grounded in the politics of dialogue.

# HOPE

It is worth making the argument that Judaism is nothing short of a sustained protest of hope. Our ancestors from Biblical times onwards overcame adversity with hope again and again. Moses addressing the Children of Israel shortly before their entry into the land issues the exclamation to "choose life." As he says, "*I call heaven and earth to witness against you this day, that I have set before thee life and death, the blessing and the curse; therefore choose life, that thou mayest live, thou and thy seed.*" (Deut 30:19). In truth it is an injunction that as Jews we have come back to throughout our history and that we must again affirm following the brutality of 7th October. The third section of essays then thread together a message of hope, urging us to hear to the voice of faith beyond the noise and spur us to action too.

A famous *midrash* (Genesis Rabbah 39:1) has it that at the outset of our ancestor's journey from his father's house, Abraham comes across a burning palace. "*Is it possible that this palace has no master?*" he asks. Whereupon the Lord Himself looks out from the palace and says, "*I am the master of this palace!*" It is at this moment that Abraham, spiritual founder of Judaism, Christianity and Islam discovers morality itself. As he sees the palace and the Master of the Universe both burning, it must therefore be up to him to extinguish those flames.

After the events of October 2023, there of course remain many unanswered questions, not least of which is how on earth such barbarity can possibly happen? I am reminded of Abraham Joshua Heschel's plea that *"mere knowledge or belief is too feeble to be a cure of man's hostility to man....The only remedy is personal sacrifice: to abandon, to reject what seems dear and even plausible for the sake of the greater truth; to do more than one is ready to understand for the sake of God"* (*Insecurity of Freedom*, p.97). Today, as the world burns, it is up to us, the children of Abraham, to douse those flames together. The voices that speak in the pages ahead are a small attempt to dampen those flames and point us in the direction of hope!

**Simon Eder**
Education Director, Louis Jacobs Foundation
*London, November 2023*

# Foreword

Hope is a word richly embroidered with meaning in English. Emily Dickinson's famous maxim that hope is, *"the thing with feathers that perches in the soul and sings the tune without the words and never stops at all"* stills us with its imagistic beauty. We use the word 'hope' often, and often more casually than we might intend. Its majesty is diminished by its ubiquity, but the concept remains. Yet, this ineffable, emotional concept of hope that Dickinson clings to is not the only, nor the best.

In the old Norse myths of the Sagas, hope (*vön*) is the slobber which drips from the jaws of Fenris, the wolf who devours the world at Ragnarok. It was this idea that prompted the cultural value of bravery even, and perhaps especially, when there was no hope of victory. Meanwhile Dante, in his Commedia, emblazons the gates of Hell with the words: *Lasciate ogne speranza, voi ch'intrate* – Abandon all hope, ye who enter here. The hope of Dante is the expectation, the belief, that the future will be better, that things will turn out well.

What is the Jewish conception of hope? Is it closer to the sanguine saliva of the world-consuming wolf? Is it more Dickinson or Dante? It is neither, I think – and I expect that's good news. Hope in our imagination is a posture, a position – it is active and engaged. As Lana Del Rey sings it, *"hope is a dangerous thing for a woman like me to have."*

Hope, in the Hebrew conception, is rooted to the idea of rope. Not just a wonderful rhyme, it is quite literally the case that תקווה and the biblical exhortation to קוה אל יי are derivatives of the verb ק.ו.ה. Also derived from this are the words for a line (as a plumb-line or rope). Interestingly, in Hebrew and all its cognates, the verb means both 'to wait for, to twist towards, to anticipate' and also 'rope, cord, twisted thread'. This is no accident – this is the conception of hope that we have.

Imagine a rope made from twisting threads together, held in place by tension and yearning – hope is to twist ourselves towards the thing we want. Just like the root is used for gathering (מקווה), hope is a feeling where we gather together the disparate threads of ourselves and then we apply pressure, then we twist. Hope is something we must do, not something we may feel.

Hope then, is a strength and an action. Is it not the delicate feathered thing of Dickinson, nor the emotion to be discarded at Dante's devilish gates. It is a thing we must do – we must gather ourselves, twist ourselves, use the tension of the current moment to help create the future we envision, the things we hope for.

קַוֵּה אֶל יְהוָה חֲזַק וְיַאֲמֵץ לִבֶּךָ וְקַוֵּה אֶל יְהוָה.

*Twist towards God – strengthen yourself and encourage your mind and twist towards God. – Psalm 27.14*

**Adam Zagoria-Moffet**
Director, Louis Jacobs Foundation
*St. Albans, November 2023*

# Preface

## Rabbi Dr. Louis Jacobs
### The Threat and the Victory

*Originally published in* The New Londoner: The Magazine of the New London Synagogue, *1:7 (January 1968).*

*This article has been included as part of our mission at the Louis Jacobs Foundation to make R' Jacobs works accessible to a new generation and to continue to model Jewish life as he did, as a quest for Torah and meaning. The book that follows was composed with that mission in mind, as Rabbi Jacobs often put it: "The quest for Torah is itself Torah."*

It has been said many times but it bears repeating: none of us can ever be the same again. When, at the beginning of June, the State of Israel was threatened with destruction, Jews all over the world and of every shade of opinion were moved spontaneously, even compulsively, to demonstrate their solidarity with Israel. In the process they discovered within themselves barely suspected depths of Jewish loyalty and commitment. The finest hour of our brothers and sisters (terms which have acquired a fresh significance) in Israel, found Jewry outside Israel ready and willing to shoulder to the full their part of the burden.

The New London Synagogue has no cause to be ashamed of its contribution. In a few days a sum in the region of £100,000 was raised as a particular Synagogue effort, to say nothing of the prominent part some of our congregants played in the general communal endeavour. A number of our young men and women volunteered for service by the side of the Israelis, returning to tell us of the wonders they had witnessed, the courage and elevation of spirit, the high morale and determination to act in a civilised manner in the face of the severest provocation. The coarseness, the immorality, the gloating over defeated foes, the urge for vengeance, all of which have in human history frequently disgraced the victors in a just cause, were almost totally absent. A distasteful task forced upon them was executed with speed and efficiency with the strongest desire on the part of everyone to get it all over with and to return to constructive work and the pursuit of permanent peace.

How should religious Jews react to what has happened and how should they interpret it in the light of their faith? It is perhaps too soon to see the Six Day War in its historical perspective but we are not absolved from considering its theological implications.

The word "miracle" has quite naturally been bandied about a good deal but what does a miracle mean in this context? Some have pointed to alleged evidence of direct supernatural intervention— the second shell which dislodged a water tank so that the water put out the fire started by the first shell, the Egyptian soldiers who surrendered their tank for no good reason to an Israeli wearing tefillin. The trouble is that tales of this kind are generally reported tales. Like the Indian rope trick it is always a case of a man who knew a man who had heard another man tell of having seen the marvellous event. And what of the many fires which were not put out until severe damage had been done and the tanks which did not surrender without loss of life? What of the skill and courage of the Israel generals and air force, of the heroism of the ordinary soldiers, of all the human ability and tenacity which made victory possible?

Some have tried to engage in the fruitless and grotesque attempt of apportioning the share in the victory between God and the human participants, as if the tremendous event could be seen in chocolate-cake terms, with so much of this ingredient and so much of that, and as if, over and above the war between the Israelis and the Arabs, there was a battle for the lion's share in the victory between God and His creatures.

A more satisfactory way of seeing the hand of God in the June war, is to see God at work not in this or that bit of deliverance but in the process as a whole. The skilful planning of the Israelis, their resistance to aggression, their readiness to sacrifice for a cause they believed to be just, the realisation that they were not fighting a war of conquest but were defending their homes and families, the age-old dream which had helped to bring Israel into existence and inspired its inhabitants to keep it in being—all these were God's instruments, as were similar ideas in the miracle of Dunkirk years ago.

Our Rabbis say, for instance, that whenever a judge gives a right decision he acts as a co-partner with God in the work of creation. They surely did not mean that the judge should neglect rigorous attention to the legal aspects of the case before him. A judge might well pray to God to help him decide correctly but he would be a poor judge if he relied on his prayers as can excuse for failing to examine with the utmost application the niceties of "the law, hoping that God would guide him to pull the decision out of the air. The judge's co-partnership with God consists in the God-given capacity for him to become expert in the law, in the knowledge and wisdom which equipped him for the lofty role he has to play, in his society's passion for justice, in the objectivity which enables a frail human being to rise above his personal emotions when truth is at stake.

Yet seeing God at work in the process is quite different from sanctifying warfare. One of the most encouraging features of the whole episode is that for all the admiration for the heroic fighters very few Jewish voices have been raised to glorify military might. The war had to be fought because the alternative was, sooner or later, annihilation. The Israelis looked upon it as a necessity but a tragic necessity, a necessary evil but an evil nonetheless. Thank God, Israel has not abandoned the ancient Jewish affirmation that, as the Rabbis put it, even though there may be times when the Jew has to wear a sword he must never look upon it as an adornment. When war came and could not be avoided without loss of innocent life and all that had been built up, the soldiers who fought were doing God's work. But as Jews they were duty bound to recognise, and they did recognise, that God's true plan for man was to be found elsewhere, in building a peaceful world and a just society.

It is no use pretending that the surge of Jewish feeling engendered by both the threat and the victory has solved all our problems. It would be nearer to the truth to admit frankly that it has created new problems, though on the whole, welcome ones. No compassionate Jewish heart would prefer to contemplate the problem of Jewish adversity. Yet problems there are and they have to be faced. What, for instance, is now to be the role of nationalism in Jewish life and how are its cruder manifestations to be avoided?

We all need to be reminded that, important though the idea of peoplehood is in Judaism, the individual counts for much and his needs and strivings must not be overlooked. Any religious assessment of the situation must acknowledge that no two human beings are alike and that each human person is created in God's image with his own portion in the Torah, his own fraction of the divine light which only he can reveal. The late Rabbi Abraham Chen was, all his life, a fighter for that interpretation of Judaism which does not neglect the role of the individual. Rabbi Chen was fond of telling this remarkable tale. It once happened that the Hasidic saint, Rabbi Levi Yitzhak of Berditchev, was observed engrossed in his prayers during the Neilah service on Yom Kippur. His disciples sensed that something extraordinary was going on. The saint prolonged his prayers, leading the congregation to unparalleled heights of devotion. But suddenly Rabbi Levi Yitzhak changed the mood entirely and went on to recite the prayers hurriedly in order to bring the day of fasting to a close. After the service he was asked to explain his behaviour and he replied that he was convinced that if he had kept at it long enough he could have brought the Messiah for it was a propitious time for his coming. But he happened to notice that in the corner there sat a devout old Jew who was so weak from the long fast that if the prayers went on for much longer would be in danger of losing his life. Whereupon Rabbi Levi Yitzhak said that it was his duty to save the life of that poor old Jew and the Messiah would have to wait!

There are also the universalistic aspects of Judaism which must not be allowed to become submerged in the justifiable enthusiasm for Jewish survival and creativity. In a sense it is true that we are all Zionists now but it would be a sad day for Judaism if we failed to continue to look outwards as well as inwards. A people serving God is to be sure the Jewish ideal but the God that people serve is the Father of all mankind. This at any rate is the teaching of the great Hebrew prophets and was the inspiration of the more sensitive Zionist thinkers who for all their political realism never gave up the ideas implicit in the notion of a "kingdom of priests." It is not paradoxical to assume that with, as we all hope, the establishment of peace and security in the Near East, the energies of the Israelis and their fellow-Jews in other parts of the world will be released to build bridges of understanding with other peoples and to explore the deeper meaning of Judaism as a faith with something to say to the whole world.

And there are the sacred sites. The soil of the holy land is sacred by association. There the prophets and sages of Israel walked and taught, there God was brought to mankind. Only those dead of soul can fail to be stirred by the last remnant of the ancient Temple glories, the Western Wall. The burial places of the Biblical heroes and heroines, even when their authenticity is in doubt, are sites capable of summoning forth some of the profoundest longings of the Jewish soul. But reverence for the past is one thing, crude ancestor worship another. Few of us would wish to see a Judaism of sacred relics, of prayers to the dead, of gross superstition and mumbo-jumbo. In the name of a refined faith, we must always be on guard against any repetition of the error of primitive religion, against which our seers fought, which locates deity in a particular sacred grove or shrine.

"Thus saith the Lord:
The heaven is My throne.

And the earth is My footstool;
Where is the house that ye may build unto Me?
And where is the place that may be My resting-place?
For all these things hath My hand made,
And so all these things came to be,
Saith the Lord;
But on this man will I look,
Even on him that is poor and of a contrite spirit,
And trembleth at My word."
(Isaiah 66: 1-2).

Our increased and fierce pride in the Jewish people must never be allowed to degenerate into chauvinism. It is a hopeful sign that the Israeli leaders as well as the rank and file have behaved so decently, in victory as well as in war. There has been little of intoxication with power and the loosing of wild tongues. But there has been, and there still is, much hope and prayer and unswerving effort to bring to birth a new era of peace and happiness to a world which has almost forgotten the taste of these precious gifts of God.

# HOME

# Reuven Firestone
*Longing for Mashiach*

From biblical days to the present Jews have longed for an end to Jewish suffering and deliverance for the world at large. It is a beautiful idea that has sustained Jews for millennia by offering hope. Messianic longing is built into the very fabric of Jewish life and thought. The core of Jewish daily prayer includes a communal entreaty for God to rebuild Jerusalem and gather our exiles from the four corners of the world to return to our sacred land, reestablish the ancient courts of justice, reward the righteous and end wickedness, restore the line of King David, and reinstate the service of the ancient Jerusalem Temple. Maimonides' thirteen principles of Jewish faith include this stirring aspirational statement: *"I believe with perfect faith in the coming of the Mashiach, and though he may tarry, still I await him every day."*

But whenever the messianic impulse has moved from aspiration to implementation, it has ended in ugliness and overwhelming disaster for the Jewish people. Messianic movements always fail. Every Jewish messianic movement in history has ended in mass-deaths and displacement of Jews, in the worst cases reaching tens and even hundreds of thousands of Jewish victims.

One unfortunate aspect of Jewish messianic movements is their frightening success in fooling Jewish leadership. Rabbi Akiva, for example, arguably the greatest rabbi of his generation, was deluded into believing that Shimon Bar Kosba (called Bar Kokhba or "star man" by his followers) was the messiah. Akiva became his promoter, publicist, and spokesperson, referring to him as the King Messiah (*malka meshicha*) through an interpretation of Numbers 24:17:

> *Rabbi Shim'on b. Yohai taught: "Akiva my teacher would expound (Num.24:17): A star will step forth out of Jacob as follows: "Koziba will step forth from Jacob." Rabbi Akiva, when he saw Bar Koziba, would say: "This is the King Messiah."*

In this passage the great warrior general is called neither Bar Kosba nor his nom de guerre, Bar Kokhba, but Bar Koziba, meaning "the liar" – another play on words that made eminent sense – but only after the overwhelming catastrophe the movement wrought. The passage continues: *"Rabbi Yohanan b. Torta said to him: "Akiva, weeds will grow out of your cheeks and the son of David will still not have come!"* (Palestinian Talmud, Ta'anit 4:5, Lamentations Rabba 2:4).

Ben Torta was right. That messianic movement ended with hundreds of thousands of Jews killed and uprooted and the utter desolation of Judea. Several others resulted in catastrophe of similar proportion, including the Jewish messianic impulse resulting in the birth of Christianity. Christian rage at those who refused to acknowledge the messiahship of Jesus and ultimately his divinity, resulted in Jewish massacres, expulsions, inquisitions, and led finally to the Holocaust.

Today we are plagued by another hopeless messianism driving the Settler Movement, established after nearly two millennia of painful exile and propelled by a messianic impulse born in the shadow of the Holocaust and nurtured by the light of the State of Israel. Too many Jews have again become fooled, like the great Akiva himself, into reading the stars and seeing signs they believe prove the inevitable arrival of messianic redemption: the Balfour Declaration, the greening of the deserts, the establishment of the State of Israel, the "miracle" of the Six-Day War, the "divine warning" of the Yom Kippur War. These are read as tarot-like indications of the messianic redemption near at hand – the *ikveta demeshikha* – "footsteps of the messiah" that should be obvious to all authentic Jews.

So why, despite all our suffering since the establishment of the State of Israel, has the messiah not finally arrived? For the messianists, the answer is clear and simple: because the Jewish collective has failed to settle the Land God promised to God's people Israel. Only when Jews occupy all the Land of Israel will suffering cease. Only then will the messiah finally come.

When messianic longing is aspirational, it offers hope and solace. But whenever it is read into contemporary events it becomes a prescription for radical measures leading to disastrous results. This has been the consequence of every activist messianic movement in Jewish history, without exception. We must not make this mistake again.

# Menachem Kellner

## The Wrath of Israel

Homer's Iliad opens with *"the wrath of Achilles."* Achilles was wrathful because Agamemnon had stolen Achilles' favourite concubine. I am a happily married Jew without a concubine, peaceable by nature, but I must open this statement with an expression of wrath at Hamas and its manifold supporters, apologists, and enablers among so-called "progressives" (in whose ranks I used to count myself).

I go to sleep worrying about our hostages and our soldiers (many of whom are close relatives and students) and wake up worrying about them. One thing I do not worry about is the resilience of the people of Israel. My wrath is assuaged by the fact that I live in a country whose population proves itself time and again to be far better than their chaotic leaders. As Joe Biden, our new hero, stated: The People of Israel Live! Indeed, עַם ישראל חי! It is the citizens of Israel who have come together in an outpouring of mutual support and help. We have not waited for the government to act effectively, but have taken the burden on ourselves. Indeed, ובחרת בחיים, we have chosen life, in the face of the horror we have suffered. Up until two weeks ago, we were told repeatedly that Israeli society was fatally fractured. Hardly!

Some rabbis urged us to read about Amalek on Shabbat. Are we supposed to ordain a biblical genocide on the inhabitants of Gaza? It is bad enough that Hamas is forcing us to join them in making the lives of the Gazans a living hell. I support the blockade of Gaza, not in order to punish the population, but in order to free our hostages. It breaks my heart, but I harden my heart when thinking of 200 hundred men, women, children, old folks, and babies, whose only crime was being Jewish, living in terror, held captive by individuals with no apparent spark of humanity. It is totally in the hands of those individuals to release the hostages and thereby end the blockade.

The Iliad ends with the sack of Troy. Hamas clearly hoped to bring about the sack of Israel. The whirlwind they have reaped will, God willing, bring about their own destruction. The Iliad's sequel, the Odyssey, ends with murder and mayhem in the very home of its hero, Ulysses. Our 2,000 year odyssey almost ended in the murder and mayhem of the Shoah, but the People of Israel Live! – we created the miracle that is Israel.

The Torah teaches that all human beings are made in the image of God. The persecution of the Jews throughout our history has taught us that human beings can destroy that divine image in themselves. The IDF doctrine of *"purity of arms"* teaches that when we must fight, we fight, but we must never destroy the divine image in ourselves. We are not Hamas – עם ישראל חי – and we will continue to live so long as we remain loyal to the divine image in ourselves, and never stop looking for it in others, no matter how hard it may be to find.

# Mark Greenspan

## Does My Heart belong in the East or West?

Making *aliyah* is not an option that is readily available to many of us. Our lives are complicated by family, health, careers, and conflicting values. But that does not mean that Israel is any less important to us or that our lives are not wrapped up in the wellbeing and destiny of Israel, its land and its people. That is particularly true in times like this.

For me, Israel is the one place I feel most at home and where I have a community with whom I share common values and beliefs. But let me qualify that statement: it is the one place I feel at home in Israel even when I don't feel completely at home there. My Hebrew is not as strong as I would like. The Israeli bureaucracy drives me wild. I find Israel's orthodox hegemony to be unacceptable. And I am deeply troubled by the conflicts that are part of life in Israel. And yet Israel is my home. And when Israel is threatened by its neighbours, I am threatened.

I am often drawn to the words of Yehudah HaLevi: *"My heart is in the East, and I am at the end of the West..."* And yet, if I am honest, I would have to admit that it would not be easy for me to *"Leave all the bounty of Spain* (America)," as the great mediaeval poet and philosopher opined. Even knowing what I know about the uncertainties of Jewish history in hundreds of lands and millenia, I am not willing to ignore the power of this moment living in America and the opportunities that I have. As a result I live in a constant state of uncertainty, neither completely at-home in America nor completely at-home in Israel.

My heart is in the east when I am in the west and my heart is in the west when I am in the east. Maybe that is what it means to live in a state of *galut*, of exile, today. *Galut* is the uncertainty of not knowing where one belongs. And it is the knowledge of realising that no place is without its inherent difficulties.

There is no *Gan Eden*, Garden of Eden, for our people, anywhere. What does it mean to say that Israel is *Reishit Tzmichat Geulateinu*, the first blossoming of our redemption, when missiles are falling and my brothers and sisters in Israel are facing difficult choices?

At the present moment I feel helpless and torn, my heart in the east while I dwell safely in the west. Attending prayer vigils and donating money seem so small and meaningless. I call family and friends to offer support. And I speak out. Maybe there is something, as a Diaspora Jew, I can do to be an ambassador, not only for the state of Israel but as a representative of the best values of Jewish life.

# Ben Rebuck

## *The Ramp*

There's something special about the ramp.

Anyone who has stepped off the plane at Ben Gurion knows the signifier that you've arrived. It's the most instagrammed place in the whole of *Eretz Israel*, the proof needed to show the world you have arrived, but it doesn't just affirm your physical presence, but also the profound sense of coming home that permeates the air.

While some may see the building's design as a mere coincidence, to me, there's a deeper significance in its construction. A ramp serves as a metaphor for the journey of life, a path that takes us both upward and downward, to highs and to lows, to ascents that challenge us and descents that offer respite. A ramp symbolises ascension, and within Judaism, the concept of 'going up' is profoundly woven into our history.

– The ascension of Enoch in the Book of Genesis, seen by many as a unique event in the Torah, where an individual ascends to be with God, transcending life and death and earth's very existence.

– The prophet Elijah, whose miraculous ascension saw him 'taken to heaven in a whirlwind' emphasising his close relationship with God.

– Moses and his spiritual ascension of Mount Sinai to God Himself to receive the Torah.

– The act of making *aliyah*, which is literally transliterated as 'the act of going up,' symbolic of returning to the ancestral homeland and is considered a significant spiritual ascent.

So to Jews old and new, ascension is more than just a coincidence.

A ramp teaches some valuable lessons in life. In its incline, we find the perseverance to climb, and in its decline, the humility to descend. It's not just in the slope, but in the understanding that every rise and fall contributes to the richness of the overall experience.

So the ramp, to me, is home. How can it not be?

And life, like a ramp, is full of ups and downs, and teaches you to discover the beauties of the journey.

> *"Sunny days wouldn't be special if it wasn't for rain. Joy wouldn't feel so good if it wasn't for pain"* - Curtis '50 Cent' Jackson

# Paul Mendes-Flohr

*The Destiny of Our Generation*

A vicious cycle of vengeance continues to lacerate the land Jews and Arabs are destined to share (ultimately with equity and mutual dignity). The recent round of unprecedented violence primed by ruthless barbarity is a clarion call to find a way beyond the tragic impasse in Jewish-Palestinian relations.

Anthropological and moral imagination are thus the call of the hour – anthropological imagination to understand the pain and the anguish of the Other that fosters enmity and rage; moral imagination to illuminate a horizon of hope – of an "alternative reality" – to inform a political vision to forge a path for Jews and Arabs to dwell harmoniously in a land they both regard to be their ancestral and spiritual patrimony.

Acknowledging the pain of others, as Martin Buber taught, need not entail denying one's own anguish. He thus differentiated what he called inclusion from empathy. In empathy one's own concrete experience is liable to be lost in an emotional identification in the inner-word of the other. In contrast, by inclusion one lives through a common event from the standpoint of another person, without surrendering one's own felt-experience of that event– hence, conducting within one's soul, as it were, a dialogue between the contrasting perspectives.

In seeking to understand the pathology of Hamas' Satanic pogrom of October 7th, we are cognisant that explanation is not exculpation. Yet, if we are to overcome the cycle of vengeful violence, an understanding of the ruthless rage of the Palestinians bears the hope of extinguishing the fire that enflames the inveterate hatred of Israel.

We may take heed from the eulogy that Moshe Dayan delivered at the funeral of a member of Kibbutz Nahal Oz who was killed in April 1956 by infiltrators from the Gaza Strip.

*"Early yesterday morning Roi was murdered. The quiet of the spring morning dazzled him and he did not see those waiting in ambush for him, at the edge of the furrow. Let us not cast the blame on the murderers today. Why should we declare their burning hatred for us? For eight years they have been sitting in the refugee camps in Gaza, and before their eyes we have been transforming the lands and the villages, where they and their fathers dwelt [for centuries] into our estate. It is not among the Arabs in Gaza, but in our own midst that we must seek Roi's blood. How did we shut our eyes and refuse to look squarely at our fate, and see, in all its brutality, the destiny of our generation?"*

General Dayan had the ethical and political integrity to acknowledge that the seeds of Palestinian "hatred for us" were sown by the Zionist project. With respect to the recent Palestinian outrage, we may point to an incident of a few months ago when a West Bank settler threw a Molotov cocktail into the home of a sleeping Palestinian family, burning to death all of its inhabitants. Photographs of the charred victims of this wanton violence (censored with but muffled, hesitant words by our government), were widely televised and painfully etched in the Palestinian consciousness. Netanyahu further rubbed salt into the wound in his recent address to the United Nations, in which he defiantly exclaimed that since the Palestinians are but 2% of the world

Arab population, they should not have the right to veto any accord between Israel and Arab nations. His words were heard in Palestinian ears as a challenge to stand up and say *hineni*, here we are, we refuse to be by-passed – which could very well have been a spark that ignited the launching of the meticulously planned assault of October 7th.

Again, explanation of the pathology of the Palestinian pogrom of Simchat Torah is not exculpation, but it should prompt us to pause before casting it as a yet another savage manifestation of the Gnostic disease of antisemitism that has haunted the Jewish people for time immemorial.

# Francis Nataf

*Finding God's Benevolent Hand*

The current conflict with Hamas finds me overwhelmed, bewildered and not sure where to focus. And yet since many expect me to convey something profound – or at least comforting – I will attempt to put forward something helpful:

Like many people of faith, I yearn to see God's presence in the world. And like most religious Jews, I see the return to Jewish statehood as an expression of that presence. It is relatively easy to see God in our nation's great victories. More difficult is to find Him in the apparent setbacks of the Jewish return to Zion. And yet the Jewish tradition endorses looking for God's benevolent hand even in such circumstances, and not just as a prod to repent. In this context, I have often discussed how fundamental this is to Rabbi Akiva's thinking on how Jews are truly meant to look at history.

Hence I want to suggest at least one (I believe there are actually many) positive development coming out of this war that – short of open miracles and/or suspending human free will, both of which go against the rules generally assumed to be central to how God runs the world in our times – was otherwise basically impossible. Some will no doubt disagree with my analysis and others will disagree with the project altogether.

To the former, I would say that this is merely an example of the type of thinking needed to try to understand what God might be doing. Neither you nor I are prophets and we should offer suggestions with humility, knowing that we can only make educated guesses at what is behind God's thinking. So long as we are prepared to accept God taking history in a different direction than we anticipated, my experience is that many find this type of exercise very helpful.

One thing that has become clear from this war is that Hamas must be taken out of the picture. It is not that we did not know that they were intent upon the destruction of the Jewish state. Rather the calculation was whether they could be contained at a lower cost than would be borne by having to uproot them. A large part of the cost had to do with international tolerance of such an operation. Determined American opposition to such a campaign in the past could well have led to Israel's ostracization, something that would have debilitating economic repercussions and possibly security ones as well.

The massive and brutal Hamas onslaught of Oct. 7 changed all that. It allowed the rest of the world to fully see who Hamas are and what they want. As a result, Israel has finally been given a free hand to get the job done, following President Biden's and other Western leaders' unequivocal call for Hamas's destruction. This is not to even mention the uptick in the all-important wall-to-wall Israeli resolve to do this, in spite of the sacrifices it will almost certainly require.

Human beings are generally not in a position to sacrifice lives in the short term in order to save many more lives in the future; that is something that requires a calculation that only God can make. It could be that He has.

As historical events like this have the potential to challenge our faith, we must understand that part of what God wants from us is to seek His loving hand even in the face of tragedy and sorrow. Whether I have located it or not, however, I am convinced that God's loving hand is very much with us.

# David Golinkin

*"Do Not Stand Idly by the Blood of Your Fellow"*

In the weekly portion of *Lekh Lekha*, Abraham's nephew Lot, his family and possessions are taken captive. Abraham and his retainers immediately pursue them all the way to Dan and rescue all the people and possessions (Genesis 14:12-16). In other words, Abraham fulfilled the mitzvah of *"do not stand idly by the blood of your fellow"* (Leviticus 19:16).

From this verse, our Sages learned that a Jew must save the life of a fellow Jew who is drowning or being attacked by robbers (Sanhedrin 73a). This halakhah was later included as Mitzvah No. 237 in Sefer Hahinukh written in 13th century Spain.

Since the dreadful attacks against thousands of innocent civilians on Simhat Torah, we have witnessed an entire people in Israel and the Diaspora emulating Abraham and fulfilling this *mitzvah*: hundreds of soldiers, policemen and civilians died in order to save others from slaughter; hundreds of thousands attended funerals and shivas; hundreds of thousands are helping soldiers and uprooted civilians; hundreds of thousands are harvesting crops, giving blood and volunteering; the State of Israel is doing whatever it can to free the hostages; and the Jews of the Diaspora have donated hundreds of millions of dollars and tons of equipment to help Israeli soldiers and civilians.

In other words, the Jewish people has once again proved the words of Rabbi Isaac Abarbanel (to Judges 21:5): *"All the good of Israel and their survival depends upon their being united."* Together, we will win!

# Eliezer Diamond

*Where Can We Find Holiness?*

We call Israel *Eretz ha-Kodesh*, the Holy Land. The most profound and well-known symbol of holiness in Israel is the Kotel, a section of the retaining wall constructed by Herod to surround and support the plaza on which the expanded Second Temple stood. For some of us, this is the place where one has the most profound sense of connection with God and, through that, a deep experience of the holiness of Jerusalem and the Land of Israel as a whole.

This form of holiness is what I call vertical holiness. The holiness flows from God above and is received by humanity below. In other words, we are swept up into a transcendent experience.

There is, however, a horizontal expression of holiness, which underlies the notion of being a holy nation. This holiness has elements of transcendence as well.

Living a holy life as part of a community requires the cultivation of two character traits. The first is self-restraint, which is often seen as a component of the second – generosity. In part, holiness means withdrawal. When I restrain my impulses, I make space for those around me. My desires do not become a reason for taking that which belongs to others or for treating them badly. Once this space is created, I can fill it not with selfishness but with generosity. This is an expression of a different aspect of holiness: transcendence.

I am well aware that greed, selfishness, violence, and injustice in

Israel as there is everywhere else in the world. Nonetheless, I see Israel as a daring experiment and a unique opportunity. Can we create a holy community in a Jewish state, however imperfectly?

No doubt, some would say that Israel is very far from reaching that dream. I choose to see those aspects of Israeli society that point towards holiness. Generosity, especially in difficult times, is strongly rooted in Israeli culture, as is all too obvious in this difficult moment in which Israel finds itself. That generosity includes the willingness to put oneself in harm's way in order to protect both one's fellow citizens and the state as a whole.

Israelis, for the most part, are aware that the country they live in is a fulfilment of an age-old dream. Therefore, maintaining and supporting the State of Israel is not just an existential necessity; it is the fulfilment of a promise made long ago, a fulfilment which required – and requires – effort and sacrifice. Again, the present is transcended to acknowledge the past and its importance.

I think that Rabbi Shlomo Zalman Auerbach drew upon this understanding of Israel's holiness when he remarked, *"When I feel an urge to stand at the graves of the righteous, I go to Har Herzl and stand at the graves of the soldiers who gave their lives in defence of the Jewish people."*

May Israel always be a place in which a holy nation does the holy work of living each day as a fulfilment of a mission, a mission that is realised through everyday life but also transcends it.

# David Mevorach Seidenberg

## *The Second Clause of the Covenant*

Avram/Avraham is promised the land we call Israel four times, all in *parashat Lekh Lekha*. The first time is Gen. 12:7, then 13:15, 15:18, and finally 17:8. But inside the promise to give Avram the land is another implicit promise: do injustice, betray the poor, attack the stranger, mistreat the land, and God promises to expel you from the land. This is implicit in the darkness that comes between the second and third times that God gifts the land to Avram.

Avram is told: *"Your seed will be a stranger in a land not theirs...for the sin of the Emorites is not yet full"* (15:13). We learn from this that the Emorites still rightly possess the land, and it is sin that is destined to bring their expulsion from the land, not any promise to Avram. This clause becomes part of the promise to Avraham's children too: whenever they possess the land, whatever the promise, they can be expelled if they miscarry justice. It is a promise that becomes explicit in other books of the Torah and Prophets.

Further on, in 21:34, Avraham is described as sojourning many days, not in "his" land, but in the land of the P'lishtim – in the name now equated with Palestine. Avraham clearly internalises this lesson. When he comes to bury Sarah in *Chayei Sarah*, he describes himself not as the rightful inheritor of the land, but as *ger v'toshav* – a *"stranger and temporary settler"* (23:4).

The Torah likewise teaches that we are all *"strangers and temporary settlers"* (Lev. 25:23). It is a privilege to live in the holy land, not a right – a privilege that can be revoked when people abuse either the land or other human beings. In fact, it is that very fact – that everyone's tenure is tenuous – that makes Canaan/Israel/Palestine a holy land. The obverse is also true: if it ever feels like we are in a zero-sum game, where zero represents not losing but annihilation, Genesis presents exactly the opposite picture: Avraham and his children can and do live together with the people of the land.

If a person were to present themself at a family's home, saying, my family lived here a hundred years ago, please leave and let me move in, they would be laughed at. Yet the Jewish people say exactly this if they insist on displacing the Palestinians in order to inhabit the land of the promise. The only reason our claim has any meaning at all is that we and a lot of Christians and Muslims believe that our covenant still gives us a right to return to the land.

I write this as a Jew whose Gidau (great-grandfather) was a Yerushalmi of Palestine. But even with that right, Rav Kook taught that the only way in which the Jewish people could come back to the land was through purchasing land fairly, not through taking away someone else's home, but through peaceful means only (*Ma'amrei R'iyah*). This, he said, was the fulfilment of *"Love your neighbour as yourself"* – not just with individuals, but with other nations.

If the covenant is real, then the second clause of the covenant is also real: commit injustice, fill up your quota of sin, and the land will vomit you out. That is what extremist West Bank settlers are doing when they attack Palestinian villages, when they burn olive trees, when they shoot and kill Palestinians harvesting olives, when they kill sheep belonging to Palestinian shepherds. All those things are happening and have happened repeatedly. And I fear that is what Israel is doing when it carries out attacks on Gaza that lead to heavy casualties against innocent civilians, who are also oppressed by Hamas.

In this terrible moment, our first and natural desire in response to October 7 is to seek retribution and wipe out Hamas, but we cannot let ourselves forget the second clause of the covenant.

If the covenant is real, the second clause must be fulfilled. And if it is not real, then we had no automatic right to restore our nation in the first place. There is a third clause to the covenant: even if the people are exiled again, if they humble their hearts, God will return the people to the land (Lev. 26:34). May Hashem grant us strength to make a preemptive strike for justice by humbling our hearts now.

# Nathan Lopes Cardozo

## A *Perpetual Murmur* (Excerpted)

The disastrous situation in which Israel finds itself at this hour asks for serious self-reflection on a level unfamiliar to many of us. One can surely accuse Israel's leadership and security forces of failure to intercept the intentions and plans of the brutal Hamas terrorists who killed, raped, put at fire, brutally beheaded children and babies and kidnapped Israeli citizens on such a large scale. But many of us feel there is much more at stake.

How a terrorist group is capable of taking on a powerful army and entering Israel without any difficulties and without anybody spotting them is bizarre. The situation is mind-boggling and beyond belief. Burials are taking place around the country. The continuous pain and danger is unimaginable. The state is trembling on its pedestals. Until now, nobody seems to know what actually is going on and what needs to be done. The government appears lame. Not only is this war unprecedented, but it is completely unfathomable and defies all logic.

Sure, in a matter of time when things hopefully calm down and some kind of security will be re-installed, some of our leaders will start to explain what actually happened and argue that looking back, all makes sense. But it will not suffice. Our deepest instinct tells us something else is going on, which like a wave of intuitive awareness, draws us into a state of mind we normally do not experience. Like a subconscious blink that kicks in and settles in our minds and keeps knocking on the door of our consciousness, we hear a perpetual murmur from the waves beyond the shore. It is as if Israel is confronted with a kind of metaphysical crisis, an ontological emergency which touches on the supernatural. This war feels as if it is striking at the very existence of the Jewish people. As if a bomb has exploded in the middle of Israel's *raison d'etre*.

In Israel, history and revelation are one. Only in Israel do they coincide. While other nations exist as nations, the people of Israel exist as a reminder of God's involvement in world history, even when it pays a heavy price. Even Martin Buber, who did not conform to a traditional Jewish lifestyle, wrote that only through Israel is humanity touched by the divine.

Throughout its short history, the State of Israel has gone through the most mysterious events modern man has ever seen. After an exile of nearly 2,000 years, during which the old Israel was able to survive against all historical odds, Jews returned to their homeland. There, they found themselves surrounded by a massive Arab population that was and is incapable of making peace with the idea that this small mysterious nation lives among them.

Simultaneously and against all logic, this nation builds its country as no other has done, while fighting war after war. What took other nations hundreds of years, it accomplished in only a few. While bombs and *katyushas* attack its cities, and calls for its total destruction are heard in many parts of the world, Israel continues to increase its population, generate unprecedented technology, and create a stronger and more stable economy.

But all this will not be of any avail if Israel does not recognize its most outstanding characteristic: its universal mission.

We must shoulder the burden of our own singularity, which means nothing less than fulfilling our role as God's witness by way of morality, the institution of Shabbat, and the food we eat. And we must draw strength from this phenomenon, especially in times such as ours when Israel's very existence is again at stake. Once Israel recognizes its uniqueness, it will, paradoxically, enjoy security and undoubtedly be victorious. Israel is not only fighting for its soil but also for its soul.

Israelis must learn that they are first of all Jews. Not just a nation that speaks Hebrew. Our very being is a refusal to surrender to normalcy, security, and comfort. We are the most challenged people under the sun. Our existence is either superfluous or indispensable to the world. It is either tragic or holy to be a Jew (A.J. Heschel). To see our existence as tragic is suicide; to see our task to be a holy people is our future and our joy.

We need to decide. Perhaps this terrible war, with its many victims, will turn out to be a blessing in disguise. Perhaps the infighting among the different parties about the government and the High Court will come to an end. Perhaps the Jewish people will finally wake up and understand its own greatness. And enjoy its future.

# Marc Soloway
*Israel Reflections*

Walking through the Baka neighborhood of Jerusalem on Shabbat, with its narrow streets named after the Twelve Tribes and other Biblical figures amidst the sights, sounds and smells of Shabbat, has always filled me with *oneg*, a very particular type of joy. Being there on the first Shabbat of November 2023, *parashat Vayera*, was familiar and beautiful, yet profoundly different in important ways. This Shabbat was at the end of a last minute Israel solidarity mission less than a month after the horrific and brutal slaughter and kidnapping by Hamas on October 7th.

The whole country is in a state of trauma, grief and fear, which is palpable. I walked to Kehillat Hakel that Shabbat morning, a traditional egalitarian minyan. The prayers and melodies were all familiar, but the mood was different. *Vayera* contains the harrowing story of *Akedat Yitzhak*, the binding of Isaac.

The person who read this section of the Torah chanted in a guttural, Yemenite trope and when he got to the actual narrative of a man being asked by God to sacrifice his son, his voice cracked and he had to pause as tears rolled down his cheeks; so moved was he, and all who were listening, by the painful resonance of the ancient text.

When he went back to his seat, I noticed that he was next to a young man carrying a military rifle, most likely his son having a break for Shabbat from his army base by the border with Gaza.

The intense tears, I assume, are for the sons and daughters whose lives have been sacrificed in defence of Israel on the altars of war. So many children of friends and family members are serving right now, some of them just 18 years old, and their parents are full of anguish in this moment.

The previous day in Tel Aviv, after a restorative swim in the Mediterranean and its empty beaches, I sat on a rooftop with my old friend Rebecca as she received a WhatsApp message from her soldier daughter Shaya, saying *"I'm going in. No phone. I love you."* If it is not obvious, the meaning was painfully clear to this anguished mother. Shaya is a combat paramedic and, at a moment's notice, she went into Gaza. My friend immediately burst into tears. What parent wouldn't? This is the daily reality for so many here and it is unbearable. She was back out and safe after only a few hours.

At the beginning of the week, on the first day of our mission organized by the Fuchsberg Jerusalem Center, home of the Conservative Yeshiva where I studied for 2 years more than 20 earlier, we witnessed first hand the aftermath of the worst horrors in Israel's history at Kibbutz Be'eri. Around 70 Hamas terrorists entered that day and at least 130 people were murdered including women, children, babies, mostly killed in their homes – 10 percent of the population. We were the first group of civilians allowed to enter this closed military site, under supervision wearing helmets and vests as protection from rocket fire.

We saw a brutal crime scene; burnt homes, pools of dried blood and some of the knives used in the slaughter, among the scattered objects of these families' daily lives. We heard testimonies from some of the young soldiers who were the first to enter these places and witness the savage horrors. People not even in their twenties who discovered these scenes will carry the images for the rest of their lives. I too will never be able to unsee, unhear and unsmell what I witnessed a few weeks after the events. In addition to touring some of the places in the south most impacted, we also met and listened to so many different people: professors, activists, organizers, teachers, volunteers.

We spent a couple of hours with Rachel Goldberg and Jon Polin, the parents of Hersh Goldberg-Polin, a 23 year old who was at the Supernova festival, taken captive by Hamas terrorists in a pick up truck and driven into Gaza. His parents are working tirelessly for the release and for awareness of their son along with the other captives. Rachel said "I'm in shock. I'm on a mission. I'm walking through the world without a heart." They describe the situation as a global, humanitarian crisis. It is. There are 239 hostages from 33 different countries, including at least 22 Thais and people of all religions, somewhere in the Gaza Strip.

All over Israel, their faces and their stories cry out to us to help redeem them. Their families are broken and in despair and the whole country, the whole Jewish world is devastated and prays daily for their release. 1400 dead, many raped and brutalized, 239 held captive, 2000 Israelis displaced from the north and the south in temporary living situations. The whole country is also mobilised in unbelievable and diverse ways to get help where it is most needed. The left, the right, religious and secular united as citizens, *am echad, lev echad*, one people, one heart, working together and wondering what happened to their government.

On the Tuesday night of our trip we had dinner and a talk with Mohammed Darawshe, an Arab Israeli scholar and activist, who speaks intelligently and passionately about how this current war and Israeli society in general, impacts his community. The loss of innocent Palestinian life is horrific and devastating too, however much we may support Israel's right to defend its people from this evil enemy. The reaction of so many in the liberal world to call out genocide and war crimes committed by Israel while barely acknowledging Hamas' clear attempt at genocide on October 7th is beyond words.

Israel is in deep shock and mourning, anger and grief, a collective state of *avelut*, and much of the world has condemned her, us, as an evil colonising power. So many Israelis on the left, including many in the southern communities that were terrorized that day, have worked tirelessly for peace and coexistence for decades and are dismayed by the claims of so many that demonise, deny and denigrate everything about Israel. So many on the left in Israel are feeling betrayed, abandoned and confused.

My few days in Israel at this awful time has left me in no doubt how strongly I stand with Israel, for all the failures of its government and prejudices of some of its people. If I was not needed elsewhere right now, I would have stayed, to be right there with my people in their pain and also in their resilience and hope. Every single person I interacted with and hugged in these few days thanked us for coming and expressed how much the support means to them.

Mohammed Darawshe reminded us that in Muslim tradition, Abraham takes not Isaac as a sacrifice, but his other son, Ishmael. So many sons and daughters are being sacrificed right now and it is excruciating. The *parashah* that I heard chanted so tearfully in Jerusalem has a repeating motif of lifting and opening eyes to see something that may have been there all along, or may have just appeared at the last moment. Abraham lifts his eyes and sees three people who turn out to be angels and he greets them. He lifts his eyes again to see the place from afar on which he is being asked to sacrifice his son Isaac; and again he lifts his eyes and sees the sacrificial ram caught in a thicket by its horns that saves the life of his son. Hagar, banished into the hot desert with her son Ishmael close to dying of thirst, has her eyes opened by God and she sees a well of water and gives her son to drink and saves their lives.

Angels weave their magic all over these texts and allow us to see what was not possible a moment before. We cannot give up hope that the children of Abraham, Ishmael and Isaac and their descendants, will one day be able to lift their eyes and see another way, a way of peace in the form of a different kind of sacrifice and no more sons and daughters dying on the altar. As much as I yearn for that day, for a universal, prophetic dream of peace and coexistence, right now my heart is broken by what I have seen and how the world spins it in ways that unleash hateful and ignorant rhetoric against us. I want to see Israel heal, survive, flourish and rebuild. *Am Yisrael Chai.*

# Miriam Feldmann Kaye
## *Bearing Witness*

We stand today as witnesses.
As living testimony, while events unfold.
At this very moment, we bear witness to the absence of all sound,
of speech,
even of tears, during the minute's silence
      marking the time since the massacres.
The still, small voice, faint, mute, hard to decipher, expresses our
      collective incredulity at the scenes of destruction.
And yet, as witnesses, we know we must speak out, we must seek out
      some expression of the reality, as it manifests itself.


We are witnesses to the horrors of the October 7 massacres.
We are the 'generation of October 2023'.
We bear witness to the bravery,
      courage and kindness of those who saved others.
Your hostages are our hostages.
We are you.
We are Kisufim,
We are Netiv ha-Asarah,
We are Sderot,
We are Be'eri – the wellspring of hope.


We can almost hear the music of trance,
      and envision the dance, at the Reim festival.
May your silence now, in time, become your melody.
May the violence you encountered turn into your ploughshares.

The decimation of so many families chokes us,
      as the reality manifests itself.
The reality that we need to 'continue' in some way,
      while our hostages are still absent.


We are witnessing a new reality of war.
Writing from Jerusalem,
Our homes are now the home front.
We bear witness to the cacophany
      and chaos of Jewish refugees within Israel.
We become aware of their experience,
      their encounter with the angel of death,
and their Jerusalem,
Their saviour.
We bear witness to the clamour
      of displaced citizens crisis within Israel.
We have become a City of Refuge.
May you bear witness to our hospitality, to our open homes.
Our Jerusalem is your Jerusalem,
What's mine is yours,
We are you.
You are us.


In the days after the attacks, I asked myself
      whether this level of cruelty marked a failure of humanity?
Would this catastrophe crush our ideals,
      undermine the belief that we are created in the divine image?
Were we witnessing the divine regret
      for creating the world that we read in Genesis?

It is becoming apparent,
It's becoming clear,
that the divine conviction that the word should exist,
even for the sake of a minority,
was a world worth re-creating.

Even a world recovering from a flood,
Even a world recovering from the crash and ruins of the tower of Babel,
Our world, recovering from 7 October, is a world worth living,
    re-creating, and believing in.
Your regret is our conviction to rehabiliate.
We are You.
You are us.

It is a brave new world,
A world of Jewish rehabilition after decimation
    that we have experienced from time immemorial.
The people of eternity does not fear,
    even from the precipice of a very narrow bridge.

We are amazed by our ability to bear witness to new sensations.
To love those who we don't know!
To witness a deep sense of compassion for those we have never met!
We delight at the release of a hostage,
    celebrate her return as if she were our own daughter!
Their hunger is my hunger.
Their needs are my needs,

Wherever you go, I will go,
Your heroes are my heroes.
Your suffering is my problem,
Where you rest, I shall rest,

The destruction of their livelihood
        is my community's responsibility to regenerate.
Their almost barren land will yet bear fruit,
        as we go out into the orchards, the fields,
            to harvest the crops of those serving on the front lines.

May the ploughshares of Isaiah work the land,
May the burned land recuperate,
May the crops be fruitful and multiply,
May those who planted seeds in tranquility,
reap the rewards, with joy.
Where you harvest crops, I harvest.

Your people is my people.
We are Kibbutz Nachal Oz,
and Kibbutz Nir Oz.
We found the inner strength – עֹז - Oz
We found the wellspring of hope within us.

# HEAL

# David Newman
## *Between Yom Kippur and Simchat Torah*

Only thirteen days separate the most solemn day in the Jewish year, Yom Kippur, from one of the happiest days, Simchat Torah. From a day of introspection and fasting, we move swiftly to the week of Succot and the ultimate rejoicing of completing and restarting the yearly cycle of the Torah. It is appropriate that Simchat Torah always comes immediately after Hoshana Raba, the day on which the entire month and a half long process of redemption and atonement comes to an end, and the final closing of the book on the previous years wrongdoings is sealed and delivered (on Hoshana Raba), as we look forward to the commencement of the new year.

From this year on however, there will be another count – fifty years which separate Yom Kippur of 1973 with Simchat Torah of 2023. Two occasions on which the very existence and the integrity of the State of Israel was threatened by our enemies. The surprise attacks on Israel by Egypt and Syria in October 1973, just six years after the victory and euphoria of the Six Day War, threatened Israel's existence. Most of us who were alive at that time remember where we were on that Yom Kippur and how and when the news infiltrated through, especially to those of us living outside Israel, in our synagogues and during the long day of prayer. It was an unforgettable moment in the history of the Jewish people and the State of Israel.

Each year since then, Yom Kippur has been remembered in Israel for that war. The Israeli news channels are full of programmes which revisit the events of October 1973, which, in retrospect, brought about the eventual fall of the Labour Party hegemony in Israel, as well as the historic peace agreements which were signed a few years later between Israel and Egypt.

This year, as we marked the fiftieth anniversary and commemoration of the Yom Kippur War, there was a feeling in Israel that fifty years – half a century – had finally put a line under this event. Israel had moved on since that time; the majority of Israel's population were born after October 1973, and while there still remain many Israeli citizens, anyone over the age of 60, who recall the events and still bear the scars of personal bereavement, Israel had nevertheless moved on. A country which had undergone considerable economic and social development, a country no longer threatened with an existential threat, not least in the years following the signing of peace agreements with many of the Gulf States and, so it appeared, an agreement being worked out with Saudi Arabia.

The Palestinian issue remained a major problem — the Hamas takeover of the Gaza Strip continued to threaten the daily peace of Israel's communities and residents of the south of the country, but not in any form or fashion which threatened the stability or existence of a thriving and dynamic State. If anything, the threat with which we have been concerned during the past year was very much an internal one, the rise of an extremist right wing government, the attempt to change many of the basic building blocks of a thriving democracy, an internal indulgence which assumed the almost complete disappearance of the external and existential threat.

And then we woke up to the events of 7th October, as we celebrated

Simchat Torah. Not only did the "enemy" once again use the surprise of a Jewish festival, when people were celebrating, be it in the synagogues with the *Sifrei Torah*, or be it in the open air music parties in the vicinity of the Gaza Strip. The last thing on anyone's minds was the idea that this sense of peace and relative stability could again be threatened, as it had happened fifty years previously.

This time the threat was not one which was eventually fought out in the territory of neighbouring countries (Syria and Egypt). This time the threat came inside the very homes and families of the Jewish people, events which the very *raison d'etre* of the State of Israel was meant to have prevented. "Never Again", not the Holocaust and neither Masada, were the slogans which we attribute to the State of Israel and its ability and readiness to prevent Jews being slaughtered and massacred in their homes – which was precisely what happened on that fateful day just a few weeks ago. The subsequent events, which continue at this very moment of writing, may indeed have brought about a renewed sense of Jewish unity within Israel, the idea that we all – religious and secular, right and left wing, are in the same boat of a world which in "every generation seeks to kill us" but it was a price, the final cost of which is still unknown, which is too large to bear, and one which, like the Yom Kippur War, will be remembered every year on this day for the next fifty – and even longer – years in the history of the State of Israel.

We say the Yizkor prayer on four occasions during the Jewish year – on each of the three festivals of Succot (Shmini Atzeret-Simchat Torah), Pesach and Shavuot and on Yom Kippur. The reciting of Yizkor on Yom Kippur in Israel has, for the past fifty years, been strongly associated with the over 2000 soldiers who were killed during the 1973 War. But they were all soldiers, not women and children, babies and the aged and disabled, who were massacred in their homes, something which even in our wildest dreams we could not have envisaged happening.

From this year onwards, the reciting of Yizkor on Simchat Torah (which in Israel is on the same day as Shmini Atzeret) will forever be associated with the thousands – we do not yet know the final figure – who were murdered and slaughtered in the largest (and we hope only) pogrom of the 21st century. Yizkor is a prayer which is more appropriate for the solemnity of Yom Kippur, than it is for the celebrations of Simchat Torah. How exactly this remembrance will take place in future years is uncertain, especially amongst those for whom the day is one of religious joy and celebration. How will the parents, siblings, children of those murdered commemorate the happy day of Simchat Torah? What will be the nature and content of the special prayers of remembrance which are yet to be composed, to be added to the lamentations of Tisha B'av, and to be inserted in the Simchat Torah prayers at the time of Yizkor? It is far too early yet to know – but it will take far longer than the fifty years and thirteen days which separate Yom Kippur of 1973 and Simchat Toah of 2023, to ease the terrible sense that the State of Israel did not live up to its ultimate objective – of ensuring the safety and peace of the Jewish people.

Yom Kippur and Simchat Torah – two days so close to each other in the Jewish calendar, two days which will forever be separated by fifty years, two contrasting days on which we will recite the Yizkor prayer and remind ourselves of the fragility, but enduring existence, of the Jewish people.

# Dalia Marx
## *The Steadfastness of the Civil Society in Israel*

The attack that took place on October 7th surprised us, left us unprepared, in more than one way, similar to the the situation regarding Yom Kippur War, which broke out exactly fifty years and a day prior. With a thrust of a knife, the history of the State of Israel was sliced in two – before and after.

The murderous attack, which took place on the holiday celebrating the Torah (Simchat Torah), on the day we begin to reread our holy book and recall the creation of the world, resulted in the violent deaths of more than 1400 men, women, children, babies and the elderly, 241 abductees, thousands of wounded and an entire country bleeding and thunderstruck. Not only the unimaginable loss of human life - hundreds of young people who danced at a peace party, many hundreds of residents who lived a calm and quiet existence within the borders of the State of Israel, a life of justice and quest for peace, and hundreds of soldiers and policemen who came to protect them, not only the outburst of absolute evil and sadism - but also, what is known today in Israel as the "collapse of conception."

The collapse of the conception is the realisation that we did not understand, that we were not prepared adequately, that we "fell asleep on our watch" as the military phrase says, that our formal leadership did not heed many internal and external warnings. However, not only did the concept collapse, but also on a mental and emotional level – when you hear about the horrific atrocities it is hard to believe that human beings, human beings like you and me, could engage in them. The human psyche, the human mind refuses to believe that such evil is possible.

When we hear about an array of hundreds of kilometers of underground tunnels built by Hamas in Gaza, it is hard to understand why this terrorist organization chose to invest all the enormous sums at their disposal in building a terrorist network and not in rebuilding Gaza, which could have been a real Middle Eastern gem, with its beautiful beach and desert landscape. Why did Hamas choose to focus its ability on attacking Israel, rather than choosing the welfare of its people? Is it really possible to hate the enemy so much, to hate him even more than loving your people and their well-being?

Philosophical questions about the absolute evil of Hamas on the one hand, and questions about the incompetence of the Israeli leadership on the other, troubles Israelis today. But we can't indulge in them too much, because we don't have the time for them. Everyone's hands are busy repairing, helping, volunteering, contributing.

Where the official leadership has failed, the firm and steadfast Israeli spirit has emerged – with countless organizations, communities and individuals helping the evacuees, supporting the families of the hostages and demanding their return, assistance to the families of reservists, huge fundraising efforts, taking part in cooking, caring for children, setting up educational programs for young people and mental health assistance for those with difficulties, harvesting and caring for livestock in kibbutzim that were affected.

Civil society in Israel has discovered (at an unbearable price) its enormous power! It is this that allows us optimism even in the difficult situation in which we find ourselves.

We will get through this crisis, and the war will end, and may it end as soon as possible. We will no longer be what we were before October 7th, but, I believe, we will be better, more compassionate, wiser and more just.

*May the Eternal grant might to God's people;*
*may the Eternal bestow on God's people with peace (Ps. 29)*

# Jane Liddell-King

## *Israel in Crisis*

I can't imagine the anguish felt by Jake Marlowe's family as they buried their son on Tuesday, 17<sup>th</sup> October. A security guard at the Supernova Trance music festival, he had been killed aged just 26. I can't imagine the pain that drove Thomas Hand, father of 8 year old Emily, to call the news of her murder at their kibbutz on 14<sup>th</sup> October "an absolute blessing" by comparison with what he feared would have happened to her as a hostage in Gaza.

I can't imagine the anguish experienced by those families plunged into sudden grief and forced to relive images of burnt and beheaded bodies. I can't imagine the endless fear and helplessness that goes with not knowing if a kidnapped relative is still alive and suffering intolerably.

For many of us, the scenes of the massacre of 7<sup>th</sup> October recall the Holocaust and pogroms also aimed at Jewish extinction. Even as I recognise my inability to imagine the pain of others, I acknowledge the obligation to go on trying, to enact the single *mitzvah* of *Vayikra* 19:18:

לֹא-תִקֹּם וְלֹא-תִטֹּר אֶת-בְּנֵי עַמֶּךָ, וְאָהַבְתָּ לְרֵעֲךָ כָּמוֹךָ: אֲנִי, יְהוָה.

*You shall not take vengeance or bear a grudge against your countrymen. Love your fellow human as yourself.*

Martin Buber reads this verse as a continuation of the previous one:

לֹא-תִשְׂנָא אֶת-אָחִיךָ, בִּלְבָבֶךָ;
הוֹכֵחַ תּוֹכִיחַ אֶת-עֲמִיתֶךָ, וְלֹא-תִשָּׂא עָלָיו חֵטְא.

*You shall not hate your relative in your heart.*
*Reprove your neighbour but don't incur guilt because of him.*

He perceives how "real responsiveness" demands taking "real responsibility" The alternative of wounding another inevitably wounds oneself (*Between Man and Man*, 1944).

How did Buber respond to his Arab neighbours in Jerusalem? In 1942, he founded *Ihud* (Unity) which proposed a bi-national state based on equal political rights for Jews and Arabs in an undivided Palestine. Outspoken opponents of bloodshed and destruction, the vision of the group was destroyed by the political facts of the late 1960s.

But how is understanding to be reached today? How do we resist branding an entire population as terrorists, blinding ourselves to people attempting to live ordinary lives?

In 2008, I met in Brussels, Professor H, a Holocaust survivor, a scientist, who, together with colleagues had responded remarkably to the fact of being alive. The group determined to fund young Palestinians to study for doctorates at Belgian universities. Our meeting had been engineered by Dr K, one of these recipients.

While our paths crossed in Cambridge, he had always turned away. But then he overheard me using the phrase: 'survivor guilt'. "I suffer it," he confided, "every single day."

His first words to Professor H. at Brussels Airport had been: "Now I want to meet the enemy, the Jews of Belgium."

"We'll see what we can do," replied his host, "you might like to start with me."

Currently, we are suffering waves of antisemitism, of inane chanting: "From the river to the sea." Our posters of the kidnapped are ripped down.

Israeli soldiers await the order to invade Gaza for the impossible task of destroying not people but an ideology.

Hope surely lies in meeting with those suffering the violence resulting from Hamas' uncompromising mission to wipe out Israel and in finding ways to offer support.

The dead and dying on both sides demand more than the exchange of words. And if not today, when?

# Naomi Graetz

## Command Centres, Compassion, and Chamas

Two weeks ago, when the war broke out, I kept on hearing people talking about *chamal* – חמ"ל – and didn't quite understand what it was. I tentatively asked my husband, is that an acronym for war room – *cheder milhamah* חדר מלחמה? You might wonder, how after more than 55 years in the country, with fluent Hebrew, I had never been aware of this?

Well, there was never any need. But today, all you have to do is turn on the television and what you hear is that there are hundreds and maybe more (and I am not exaggerating) *chadrei milhamah* (plural).

What is a *chamal*? Let's say that you are not sure if a relative of yours, let's say your son, is missing since October 7th when he went to the party with another 3000 people. Someone said they may have seen him laying (possibly dead) next to his friend, who has been identified via DNA, but they have not gotten any official notice about their own son.

They organise a *chamal*, which consists of friends, soldiers, anyone with connections. They make phone calls, scour Facebooks, go to hospitals, to the morgues dealing with forensics. They reconstruct the scene and if they are "lucky" they get an answer (definite death or possible kidnapped dead or alive). For each of the 600 plus missing/kidnapped and unidentified there is a *chamal*.

This is all being done by volunteers, many of whom are bringing their professional skills to help their group. Then there are other *chamalim*, which have gotten a lot of publicity. These deal with the massive amounts of contributions given to the evacuees from the South, who arrived to "safe" places all over the country with only the shirts on their backs. Or those *chamalim* where distribution of material donated by international generosity to army bases has to be organised.

As I was thinking about the acronym *chamal*, I had an interesting association with a word with a similar sound – and that is *chemlah* which is compassion. I realized that those in these temporary command centers were acting out of compassion for people desperately in need of it. And then I thought of the word *cham* (heat) which is a component of passion, but when misused and the letter *samekh* ס is added, becomes *chamas* – which in this case is a group totally void of compassion.

I shared these fragmentary thoughts with my Buddhist daughter, Avigail Graetz, and she was shocked, how in sync we were, for just that minute she had been working on a poem, playing around with the same root—but this time having to do with war *milchamah*-- מלחמה.

We talk a bit, and I ask her to send it to me. She is fluent in Spanish and Arabic and points out to me that *chamas* in Spanish is "never again." And a word close to it in Arabic *chalas* translates to "enough." And then she sends me her poem in Hebrew.

It starts out by asking *"what kind of poetry can we write during a war?"* She plays with the roots of the word *milchamah*: *cham* (heat), *lechem* (bread), *chemah* (sympathy), *chelem* (shock and confusion).

She writes that war is complex and when we shed tears of salt (*melach*). And she ends her poem this way:

ואברהם אבינו מל.
ואפשר לחלום
על שרה והגר אופות חלה בחמלה,
מוחלות ומלחימות את הרוח שתשורר על הבנים בחמלה.

*And Abraham circumcised.*
*And we can dream*
*Of Sarah and Hagar baking challot together with compassion* (chemlah)
*Each forgiving* (mochlot) *and soldering* (malchimot)
*the spirit which will hover over our sons with compassion.*

# Herzl Hefter
*Words*

The calamity of the Yom Kippur War taught us that terrible tragedies may become opportunities for reflection. Then, as today, conceptions and misconceptions abound. It is important to examine a number of words we are hearing that require our scrutiny.

## "Vengeance"

The Torah understands that the desire for vengeance is a very potent emotion and, if not sublimated in the service of the administration of justice, will wreak havoc in society generating endless cycles of violence. That is why the Avenger of the Blood is the one who is given the opportunity to administer the punishment to the murderer, as a safety valve for the expression of vengeance. When we hear calls for vengeance, we need to be conscious of what that means. Three things about vengeance:

1) In the Torah, vengeance, whether meted out by God or by humans, is always against the perpetrators of the wrong and the guilty. If someone slaughters a family, we do not murder their family in return. We hold the murderer accountable and carry out judgement upon them. This means in warfare, we need to distinguish between the murderers and their enablers on the one hand and the non-combatant population on the other.

2) Vengeance, when it is pursued, must be devoid of self-interest. When the Torah commands vengeance, it entirely prohibits or

severely limits taking the spoils of war. At the end of the Purim story, for example, the Megillah emphasises repeatedly that the people did not partake of the spoils. The voices calling for the reoccupation of Gaza and rebuilding of Gush Katif, in addition to being dangerously disconnected from reality, undermine the moral justification for our actions. This war dare not become one of aggression but must remain one of legitimate self-defence, and shaping a more secure future.

3) Vengeance corrupts, even when necessary and virtuous. We need to take to heart the wise words of the Torah sage, Rabbi Naphtali Tzvi Yehuda Berlin (1816 – 1893). The Netziv explains why God needed to grant Pinchas a covenant of peace after his "zealous" killing of Zimri and Kosbi (Numbers 25). He wrote, "It is in the nature of the act of killing another soul to leave a traumatising imprint upon the heart. However, since Pinchas did what he did for the sake of Heaven, God blessed him that he should be at peace..."

We need to protect our souls and be mindful that our desire for vengeance does not consume us.

### "Victory"

After the terrible tragedies we have endured at the bloody hand of Hamas, what does "Victory" even mean? The destruction of Hamas is certainly a worthy tactical goal, but what are our strategic goals? The government has a responsibility to spell these out. What does the landscape look like after the dust settles and the smoke clears?

Victory is an empty word unless it is honestly defined. To what degree do some of our leaders use the word "Victory," as well as "Vengeance," to manipulate and deflect criticism from themselves?

## "Nazi"

This one is really hard. My father was the only survivor of nine children in the Shoah. He witnessed his mother being shot outside the Polish town of Sanok on the 14th day of Cheshvan 1942. Since last week I have been having nightmares. The word, "Nazi" is an obscene word, consecrated in the most unholy way. As such we must be wary not to take the name in vain.

Hamas are not Nazis. To be sure, their acts of barbarism draw comparisons to the behaviour of the Nazis. However, Nazi hatred for the Jews was pathological and nurtured by abhorrent racial theories which viewed Jews as infectious vermin that needed to be eliminated everywhere for the sake of humanity. This is not the case with Hamas – they "just" want to eliminate us in the land of Israel.

One can be very, *very*, **very** evil and still not be a Nazi. Hamas are not Nazis. Putin is not a Nazi; the Iranians and Taliban are not Nazis; our own home-grown Jewish Supremacists are not Nazis either. Neither are all evil to the same extent. We should be wary of the use of this term as a trigger or means of manipulation. It is vital for us, especially when we employ force against our enemies, to maintain a clear moral vision of their nature and the nature of their evil.

*"Holocaust"*

Allusions to the Holocaust are painful, traumatising and inaccurate. In the Holocaust we were helpless victims. A modern, militarised, technologically advanced nation state had singled us out for extermination. There was no one to protect us and we did not have the means to protect ourselves.

What happened last week was not a Holocaust. It was a deadly massacre perpetrated by bloodthirsty terrorists. It was made possible by grave tactical misjudgment by our intelligence and military establishment, by a government distracted and lacking an effective strategy of how to deal with Gaza and Hamas over the long-term. Today, we have a country of our own and an army we should be proud of – we should be able to ensure that such horrors do not happen again. Which brings me to the final word on my list:

*"Responsibility"*

With the freedom we enjoy as an independent country with considerable means to defend ourselves, comes responsibility. Mature and responsible leadership accepts responsibility to apply force when necessary, responsibility to refrain from force when not necessary and responsibility to acknowledge and accept the consequences of our failures.

Hamas does not possess the military strength to defeat the State of Israel. They know this. Their goal is to precipitate our internal collapse through the spread of fear, divisiveness and despair. We need to join together not merely united by common enemies but through our common humanity, nationhood and identity. Our moral conceptions need to be clear and our words need to reflect and express who we are.

# Miri Fenton

*Testimony from October7.org*

We are living through an unprecedented moment in Israeli history, in Jewish history. Nearly four weeks on from the massacres that Hamas perpetrated across the western Negev on October 7th, 2023, there is a palpable, growing divide between Israelis and Jews abroad. A divide in the lived experience of war and the mobilisation of all Israelis. A vastly different perspective on the rise in antisemitism across the world.

In the midst of the fallout from 7th October, social media was awash with individuals' accounts of their survival, at home, at the nature party near Kibbutz Reim, in Sderot, and across the western Negev. A small team of volunteers started working on collecting, translating, and publishing survivor accounts of their experiences that day, with their written consent. The project has grown to hundreds of volunteers, with four languages already live on the website, and significant social media presence.

While the media in Israel is still full of stories of survivors, the murdered, the missing, and the kidnapped, we realise that this is not the case everywhere. October7.org aims to confront the entire world with accounts from survivors of the massacres perpetrated by Hamas. Survivors have asked us to share their experiences as widely as possible. One example of the 120 accounts on our website is Alona T.'s story, below.

What can you do? Visit October7.org for more stories. Be in touch for ongoing educational partnerships with educational, research, and advocacy organisations. The world must know.

### Alona T.'s Story:

How did it all begin, and how did it come to an end? We arrived at the party at 4:30 a.m. The atmosphere was filled with smiles, hugs, lots of friends, and an abundance of love. Little did we know what was about to unfold.

At around 6:15 a.m, rockets began to streak across the sky, and, living in Israel, this was nothing new. Nevertheless, the events that unfolded five minutes later caught us completely off guard.

Everyone rushed to their cars, hoping to escape the incoming missiles and make their way back home. However, a massive traffic jam had formed at the entrance, forcing us to abandon our vehicle and opt for a strategy of waiting until the chaos subsided.

As we exited the car, a cry of "terrorist infiltration" pierced the air. Out of a group of six people, two friends fled, another vanished into the nearby forest, leaving only three of us behind: myself, Dana F., and my sister's fiancé. The urgency was palpable as we ran for our lives, every moment feeling like an eternity.

We sought refuge under a tree, although it provided scant cover, offering only exposed branches that failed to shield us from the relentless bullets whizzing overhead, fired by the unseen assailants. It was a cacophony of gunfire, with perhaps over a hundred bullets in the air.

Next to us we witnessed an Israeli man being captured by the terrorists, right before our eyes. He pleaded for his life, but we were powerless to intervene as he was abducted in plain sight. The ensuing screams and cries defy description, a nightmarish soundscape. The terrorists surrounded us, and we had no way of relocating from our vulnerable position. I was convinced they would discover us, certain of it.

Yet, six hours passed without any assistance. For six agonising hours, we heard nothing but Arabic and saw no signs of our own forces. We knew we were on our own, and despair set in. During this time, the terrorists began setting fire to vehicles. Fortunately, the smoke from the burning trees didn't come in our direction.

When the fire got nearer to us, we faced a harrowing decision: stay and burn or risk running, knowing that snipers could be lurking anywhere. The smoke provided some cover as we fled, managing to evade harm. Reaching another tree where other Israelis had sought refuge, we joined them and, for another hour and a half, continued to crawl, hide, and run until our rescue forces came into view.

No matter how much I recount this experience, it is impossible to convey the full extent of it without being there in the midst of it. I came [to the party] to seek solace, but I left with deeper scars, knowing that Alona would never be the same person again.

– Alona T.

# David-Seth Kirshner

*A Stream of Anxiety-ness*

Eventually, Israel will regulate its breathing and start to metabolise the indigestible. Questions will fester about failures and security breakdowns and hubris, protest movements and radical Knesset members all that precipitated the darkest day in 75 years. These are all important questions and they should and will be dealt with. But not now.

Israel will exact a crushing blow to Hamas. Like Japan's Emperor said after the airmen returned from the bombing sorties over Pearl Harbor with exuberance and pride, "Do not gloat. I am afraid we have woken a sleeping giant." Israel will pummel Hamas to a place where the glee they celebrate today will be a foggy memory. Hamas will rue the day they woke this sleeping giant.

In many ways, October 7, 2023 is worse than October 7, 1973, since the targets were primarily civilians. No Israeli was off limits. No age was a barrier. No background mattered. Women and children were ruthlessly murdered and their bodies strewn on the streets. Babies in car seats were riddled with bullets at a red light. Senior citizens barbarically murdered in cars with their lifeless bodies held up by a seatbelt. Entire families brutalised in their homes. Wounded hostages tortured and paraded about in Gaza like trophies.

And the world will surely ask us to show restraint?! To be proportionate?! In short time, they will condemn Israel! We must be armed and ready at the offensive for any print media source, cable news network, social media site or water cooler pundit who will surely try and turn the tables and reverse the narrative. We must be vigilant.

Some have said this is Israel's 9/11 moment. During those dark days in America, President Bush said, *"You are either with us or against us."* So too, there can be no ambiguity at this moment. There are no middle of the road groups here. There is no place for fence sitting. There are evil doers and peace pursuers. It is black and white.

Make no mistake. This is not about occupation. It is not an invitation to discuss land for peace or normalisation talks with neighbours. Do not get baited into that argument. This is about the undeterred focus of Hamas to annihilate the Jewish state and its citizenry. It is nothing less than old fashioned antisemitism masquerading as antizionism.

Israel and lovers of Zion will never be the same after this fateful day. But our resolve is unwavering. Our support is unshakeable. Our bond has never been tighter.

Tomorrow, Israel will awaken to the reality that is its worst nightmare. They will begin their day by once again, tilling fresh soil to bury the dead, and send teenagers to the danger zone. As they do, know that our collective hearts are now and always in the East. *L'Olam Vaed.*

*(Excerpted from the 8 October 2023 blog of Rabbi Kirshner on the Times of Israel)*

# Daniel M. Zucker

*Our Mistakes We Acknowledge Today:*
*The Oslo Accords are Dead!*

The horrific, abhorrent attack by the Islamist terrorist organisation Hamas upon southern Israel on Shabbat Shemini Atzeret-Simchat Torah, was the epitome of depravity and disdain for the civilisation that Western society generally shares in common, but which Islamist terror groups such as al-Qaeda, Isis, Hamas, Jihad Islami, Hezbollah, and the Islamic Republic of Iran all revile. The revolting, evil deeds of the Hamas invaders—all major war crimes and crimes against humanity—place them in a category of criminality that requires the ultimate penalty. We Jews despise war and bloodshed, but make no mistake, we do not share Christianity's "turn the other cheek" attitude.

Difficult as it may be, we who love Israel and crave peace, must quickly come to realise and acknowledge that we were mistaken about our abilities to bring our jihadist nemeses to the table and to forge a viable, peaceful tomorrow. We must shed our idyllic vision of an irenic future and comprehend that we and our leaders so wanted to think that peace was possible with our immediate neighbours, believing that we could teach them the benefits of co-existence, that we closed our eyes to reality.

October 7th has torn those rose-coloured lenses from off of our faces, and if we retain any degree of *seikhel*, we must see that those blinders don't return to obstruct our now clear eyesight. Make no mistake, "Pay to Slay" programs of any sort constitute genocidal war against our people.

Our enemies have stated in the clearest terms that the wish to slay us Jews—in the words of their Hadith (oral traditions ascribed to Muhammad) we are destined to suffer the following fate: "The Day of Judgement will not come about until Muslims fight the Jews, when the Jew will hide behind stones and trees. The stones and trees will say: 'O Muslims, O Abdullah, there is a Jew behind me, come and kill him.'"

Our Talmud (BT Sanhedrin 72 a-b) teaches us what must be our response to such a threat: *"Ha-ba le-horgekha, hashkem le-horgo* – If someone comes planning to kill you, arise to kill him first." October 7th demonstrates most clearly that their threat to kill us must be taken at face value and not dismissed as propaganda or hyperbole.

Israel and we Jews are the proverbial "canary in the coalmine." For Western civilisation to survive, we must convince our fellow civilised nations to join and support Israel in this hour of need as the jihadists and their supporters would not stop were they to arrive at the beaches of Haifa and Tel Aviv, any more than Hitler would have stopped had England and Soviet Russia fallen.

Just as the Nazis had to be totally defeated and their hold upon Europe completely uprooted, so must Hamas, Islamic Jihad, and any other jihadist group in Gaza be destroyed. Any and all who support jihad must be totally eradicated. If we wish to outlive the jihad plague, this policy must now be applied worldwide.

# Avi Solomon

*Two Personal Fixes: Listen to Torah, Read Maimonides*

*7 double letters, these are their transforms:*
*Death into Life, War into Peace, Foolishness into Wisdom,*
*Poverty into Wealth, Barrenness into Fertility, Ugliness into Beauty,*
*Slavery into Governance.*
  *-Sefer Yesira*

Imagine if 44,000 Americans had been murdered by Al Qaeda on 9/11. That is the true scale of the satanic pogrom of 1400 Jews in Israel executed by Hamas on 10/7.

Jews all over the world are in unfathomable throes of pain, agony and grief, but we stand together unified by one reiterated realisation: Only an truly open, deep, awake and united Judaism can provide Israel with the spiritual weapons to stand up to, defeat and flourish over her enemies.

The blinding flares of the current war against the Jews have starkly illuminated the staggering extent of antisemitism across the globe. It is now clear to every Jew that that anti-Zionism **is** antisemitism.

During this emergency, all I can share are two of my personal "fixes" (or Tikunim, Rectifications, Penances) that are helping me deal with the tragedy and function under fire:

  1 - Listen to audio of the 5 Books of Moses
  2 - Read Moses Maimonides' Letter to Yemen

Listening to the Torah is self-evident, for without the words of Moses, we are as nothing. Listen to the audio in Hebrew or Robert Alter's translation in English. Use all your spare time for it. Of course you can read the text, but that might be hard to do while stacking dishes into the dishwasher.

Maimonides was no stranger to the dismal yoke of radical Islam in his time. Reading his opening of hope to persecuted Jews in Yemen provides a healing perspective even unto our days. Two quotations from the Letter to Yemen will suffice here:

> "Never has a nation arisen against Israel more harmful than it (Islam), nor one which went so far to debase and humiliate us and to instill hatred towards us as they have."

> "All of them (Christianity & Islam) wish to imitate the religion of God (Judaism)."

This alludes to a quotation from the Talmud copied by Muhammad in his Quran:

> "If anyone killed a person, other than for murder or corruption on Earth, it would be as if he killed all the people. And if anyone saved a life, it would be as if he saved the lives of all the people."
> -Quran, 5:32

The Jewish original from the Babylonian Talmud reads as follows:

> "Whosoever destroys a single soul, Scripture imputes (guilt) to him as though he had destroyed a complete world. Whosoever preserves a single soul, Scripture ascribes (merit) to him as though he had preserved

*a complete world.*
-Sanhedrin IV.5

As Maimonides hints, the Torah given to us can never (כל) be abrogated, for it is cherished forever in our heart (לב):

> *This entire book of the Torah from the B of Bereshit to the L of Israel is the word of God to Moses our Master.*

# Art Green
## An Opportunity to Think Anew

For three weeks now, Jews everywhere have been living in the face of the most horrifying example imaginable of an anti-Jewish rampage of murderous ferocity. As I write, the Israel army is still struggling to find its proper response. The civilian public in Israel, as well as countless Jews around the world, have responded with an endless flow of empathy and generosity, stepping in when agencies of the state seem to have been paralyzed.

But how do we begin to respond religiously to such an event? What does it mean to us as people of faith, and how does the language of our tradition help us to absorb and integrate this terrible blow? Here much careful reflection will be required; that will need to take place over a long period of time. These are some initial thoughts.

I am not a Jew who believes in particular providence, in a God who consciously governs the events of history and the course of individual lives, in its conventional sense. "My thoughts are not your thoughts," says the prophet. Yes, I believe that all of existence is contained within the mind of Y-H-W-H, the eternal force of being and becoming. But that does not mean that God is "in control" of our fate in this world. We are.

Therefore I cannot formulate a question like "Why did God do this to us?" or "Why did God let this happen?" But I can – and must – ask a different question: "How can we find God in this moment? If we believe, as I do, that Y-H-W-H is to be found in every place, at all times, and in each human soul, I cannot exempt the most horrific of human moments. To search for God in the Holocaust is not to say that God caused it to happen.

We need to confront the question of evil head-on. Even if we do not think of God as doing or permitting these terrible deeds, we remain monotheists or monists. That means that everything comes from or lives within a single source, including evil itself.

The Kabbalists understood this and were not afraid to speak of it. Within the One, the forces that will potentially emerge as good and evil, angelic and demonic, are all jumbled together, just as they are in our own souls. In the deepest realms of inner reality, the distinction between them does not yet exist. But the force that drives the project of Creation as a whole, a project identical with the emergence of the One from hiding, is one of love and compassion. The world is created out of love. Ultimately, therefore hesed or compassion will triumph over sitra ahra, the "other side."

The Zohar tells us, in some of its most tightly held secret passages, that God Himself is involved in a nearly endless struggle to be freed of these inner forces of chaos and evil. Our inner struggle mirrors that of the cosmos. As we choose good and rule over the evil in ourselves, each of us makes a vital contribution to the ultimate divine triumph over evil.

Humans have freedom of choice. Our choice of which voice to follow has cosmic implications.

Those Hamas invaders chose evil in its most radical and barbarous forms. To be sure, they were acting with a full measure of divine *ḥiyyut* or life-energy within them. But they were dragging it down into its most severe abasement, rather than uplifting it to the heights of heaven, as we are enjoined to do. In doing so, they have dragged down the good name of Islam as well. True Muslims should be outraged at them. In our response to them, we must do our utmost not to become like them.

Finding the presence of God in a particular moment or situation also means attuning ourselves to listen to its message. What is the Torah of this moment? What is it that I can learn from it? Our tradition has always taught that when disaster comes upon us, we should examine our own deeds. What might we have done differently that would not have led Hamas to this terrible deed? Was there a message we did not hear? Or a warning to which we refused to listen?

In this moment, the divine voice is loud and clear: stop this circle of bloodletting. It leads nowhere but to hell. Use this moment as an opening, as an opportunity to think anew and freshly about the real question: Two peoples live in this land. Neither of them is going anywhere. How are we going to live together, rather than keep dying and killing each other?

The One who gives us life and renews it in each moment is a *ḥafets ḥayyim*. The God of life wants us to live. All of us.

# David Frankel

## A Dvar-Torah in Wake of the War in Gaza

The citizens of Israel, and the Jewish people at large, are living through a horrific tragedy, and in a state of terrible mourning. We are all suffering a mixture of pain, anxiety, deep sadness, anger, and frustration, in the wake of the barbaric terrorist operation that was carried out by religious fanatics against thousands of innocent Israeli civilians. We fear for the fate of the hostages who have been taken, and for the wellbeing of our soldiers who must embark on the perilous task of freeing them, and destroying the enemy.

As many have said, the time for recrimination and assignment of blame will come later. Now is the time for unity and resolve, for the people of Israel, and the Jewish people at large. A war of destruction has been forced upon us, and our survival depends on our coming out of it victorious. This is not about venting our anger, though anger is palpable and fully justified. Rather, we are engaged in a carefully calculated campaign to rectify an intolerable political and military situation, and to free our loved ones at the same time.

One of the most difficult aspects of the war we have embarked upon involves the terrible devastation and suffering that many innocents in Gaza will have to endure. Of course, responsibility for the death and destruction that has and will come to the people of Gaza lies squarely on Hamas, which cares much more about waging holy war against Israel than about the welfare and prosperity of the citizens it governs. Still, not all citizens of Gaza support the reign of terror of Hamas. How are we to deal with this issue on the psychological, moral and religious levels? Can we even separate our moral and religious evaluations of this matter from the psychological trauma that we are presently undergoing, or from the anxiety that we are feeling for our soldiers and hostages? Are we emotionally capable of thinking sensitively about these issues without losing our mental equilibrium, even our sanity?

Despite the difficulties, we cannot avoid the responsibility of contemplating these matters, at least on the most rudimentary level. Perhaps we may find some guidance from the famous biblical story of King David and the building of the Temple. According to the account in the book of First Chronicles (22:8), God rejected King David's request to build the Temple in Jerusalem with the words, "You have shed much blood and have waged great wars; you shall not build a house to my name, because you have shed so much blood in my sight on the earth."

In contrast with the era of David, the era of Solomon would be an era of peace. Solomon will not be a man of war and he will be spiritually fit to build the Temple. This divine statement is rather astonishing. Nowhere does the book of Chronicles, or any other biblical book, criticise David for embarking on his wars for Israel. On the contrary, the biblical books present David's wars as vital and necessary for Israel's defence, and he is basically commended for his victories on behalf of Israel! How, then, can we understand this rejection of David?

I would suggest that our tradition presents us here with a complex and paradoxical concept of great importance: there are times when it is unavoidably necessary to commit terrible sins. The fact that a terrible sin must be committed does not mitigate the fact that it is indeed sinful, and the fact that it is sinful does not mitigate the fact that it indeed must be done. This is the essence and reality of war. There is no war without the terrible suffering and death of masses of innocent human beings created in the image of God. And yet, there are times when the alternative to waging war, that is, the pacifist decision to refrain from it in order to preserve the lives of the innocent, is even worse. For to refrain from engaging in the sins of battle emboldens the perpetrators of evil and aggression to further their campaign to wreak havoc on humanity. King David fought just wars on behalf of Israel, and he is commended for that. But his hands are still stained with the blood of the innocent. His role is to pave the way for Solomon. He will build the Temple that symbolises universal, spiritual harmony.

What can we take away from this story for today? Minimally, it means that we must reject the voices of those at the extremes. Those who say that we must flatten Gaza without any concern for innocent civilians seek to refashion us in the image of our enemies. This would provide them with the ultimate spiritual victory and lead to our own moral decay. On the other hand, those who say that we must refrain from meaningful and effective military action because it would inadvertently involve the loss of civilian lives would hand military victory to the enemies of humanity, and lead to our own physical demise. Today we are living in the era of David, and, unfortunately, this means that we must sully our hands with the blood of war. But we must never lose sight of the ultimate goal. Let us pray that the resolve of our actions today will ultimately lead to the peaceful era of Solomon, and the spiritual building of the Temple in Jerusalem.

# Tzemah Yoreh
*One Does Not Judge A Person in the Time of Their Anguish*

So many of us have heard horrible things, things we can't unhear in the past few weeks, about Jews, the Jewish community, so many statements which streak past the blurry line between antizionism and antisemitism, as though it weren't there. If I were inclined to be a tweeter, I am sure some of them would have been directed at me. So far I've only been on the other end of some obnoxious Facebook comments.

As a congregational rabbi, my inbox is filled with an ever-burgeoning list of emails cataloguing these inflammatory comments and statements. At this point I don't read them anymore. I can't if I wish to embrace the pretence of a pleasant day.

I have two coping strategies: One is writing lamentations as an outlet for my bottomless grief at the tragedy that has befallen us as a Jewish community.

זֹאת קְרָאַתְנוּ וְסִפַּרְנוּ בְּשִׂגּוּן וְשָׁפַכְנוּ לֵב שָׁפוּל וְאָנוּן
מִמָּרוֹם נֶאֱלָם תַּחֲנוּן כִּי לֹא בָּא לָנוּ רַחוּם וְחַנּוּן

נַפְשִׁי אֶשְׁפְּכָה וְאֵלֶּה אֶזְכְּרָה כִּי בְלָעוּנוּ זֵדִים בְּעֶגָּה מְפוֹרָרָה
כִּי בִימֵי הַחוֹמְסִים עָלְתָה עֲבוּרָה לְאֶלֶף חֲמֵשׁ מֵאוֹת הַרוּגֵי שִׂמְחַת תּוֹרָה

*These I remember, my eyes stream with tears*
*For the evils throughout the years*
*On Simchat Torah there was no reprieve*
*Fifteen hundred were murdered, please let me grieve*

The other coping strategy is holding fast to the rabbinic principle expressed in Tractate Bava Batra '*One does not judge a person in the time of their anguish.*' What does this mean? It means that in the case of otherwise reasonable people, I refuse to judge them for their statements at the present time. I want to wait for the flames to die down a bit. I am hoping that when they do, we can have level-headed conversations.

I would like to quote a rabbinic colleague of mine, Jonathan Kligler, in a public Facebook post:

> "*I refuse to allow this war and the passionate debate surrounding it to rupture my relationships with precious family members, friends and colleagues with whom I happen to disagree. To me, that would only add to the tragedy of this moment.*"

Perhaps I can take this wonderfully compassionate thought one step farther. So many of us are disappointed in the reactions of particular people or organisations both in the Jewish world and beyond. They didn't care enough, or at all, about Jewish blood being spilled, or cared only about Jewish blood being spilled. They parroted antisemitic slogans, or were racist against Palestinians or were horribly simplistic.

We are all still reacting to a devastating trauma, and I am trying to give space for people emote, I am trying to forgive terrible things said in grief and in rage. To be very frank, I've felt tempted to say some of those same things, and were I younger, or had I lost loved ones in this tragedy, it is entirely possible that I would have. Please be kind to one another. In a time when we feel powerless, it is often all we have.

# HOPE

# Chaya Rowen Baker
*Are We Willing to Change Our Minds?*

On the morning of October 7th, after a few minutes in our bomb shelter, my family and I were preparing to leave for synagogue when the president of the congregation knocked on our door. She had come to confer whether we should hold services that morning. "*Of course,*" I said immediately. "There is a bomb shelter at the synagogue. We will restrain the Simchat Torah celebrations but this is exactly the time to pray and be together." "I'm not sure you know how bad it is," she replied. "Terrorists are driving around the town of Sderot, and 20 people have been killed."

Twenty people murdered in a terrorist attack! The number brought back memories of suicide bombings. Indeed, it was horrid. By evening we were shocked to learn that the number of people murdered was likely going to exceed the number of soldiers killed in the Second Lebanese War – 121. I am not sorry we held services that morning. They were meaningful and strengthening. I do regret using the word "celebrate" in writing to colleagues that night, saying that it was right to celebrate Torah even in hard times. I simply did not know. The horrific details of the attack – its scope and viciousness – took time to unfold. As the proportions of this atrocity continued to be revealed, I found it hard to fathom the blindly unchanging attitude of our critics. How could those who condoned the attack on October 7th not adjust their response in the slightest, in the light of what became known by October 14th? Do information and reality really bear so little weight in moulding opinion?

As more information comes to light we do see politics in Israel shifting. Classical "Right" and "Left" are wavering. While obviously not all change is desirable, I suggest that we think of shifting one's opinion as hope-inspiring. It indicates a change of paradigm, that may open up new possibilities.

The biblical verb for changing one's mind stems from the same root as the word נחמה (comfort, consolation), as in Genesis 6:7: "כִּי נִחַמְתִּי כִּי עֲשִׂיתִם" ("for I regret that I made them"). The Rabbinic verb for reconsidering is נמלך, from the same root as מלך (king). Our heritage conveys the important message that flexibility of thought and ability to change paradigms are Heavenly traits, charged with connotations of leadership and consolation. Israel is not what it was on October 6th and never will be again. Unimaginable loss and grief and horror are producing new leadership, newfound responsibility, and a renewed sense of peoplehood in Israel and around the world. Those who will wisely formulate a new vision for Israel, combining what we now know and what we still hope, without succumbing to fear and propaganda, will change it for the better.

Would that those who have condemned Israel would come forth bravely and say, "I regret what I said on October 7th. I just did not know." Thoughtful people hopefully will put aside old paradigms, acknowledging that new information should affect how we think and help identify pure evil. I also hope we all recognise that radical change is possible – indeed, the concept of change contains a measure of the Divine – and that horrific realities can inspire systemic change. Observing what has become of Germany since World War II and of Israel's relationships with Egypt and Jordan are proof of that. Achieving the impossible is part of the Israeli ethos, as is annihilating pure evil. I pray that we live up to both parts of this ethos in these most trying times.

# Avi Strausberg
## *The Imperative of Hope*

The recent events of the war in Israel have been world-shattering, bringing with them unthinkable horrors and catastrophic despair. We struggle to go through the motions of our lives, and to understand our roles and responsibilities in this crisis. In some moments, any pretense of continuing on has been impossible. The despair is just too much; the fear of ever-increasing casualties cannot be ignored. We feel such helplessness that we can imagine no positive outcome. In these moments, I have found myself simply beyond hope. I see no way forward, only a continual spiral toward darkness and terror.

Rabbi Kalonymous Kalman Shapira's Torah of faith and hope broke through the despair of the Warsaw Ghetto, teaching that hope is non-negotiable. In 1942, he wrote, "A person needs to hope at every moment to be saved by God."[1]

Whatever the depth of our despair or the terrifying facts we face, he insists, we must hold on to hope. In *parashat Hanukkah*, he taught, "faith is the foundation of everything."[2] Without faith, we are torn from God; we have nothing. For Rabbi Shapira, even when we are already in what feels like a living hell, it's losing faith and giving in to hopelessness that are the real Gehenna.

The Israeli poet Yehuda Amichai wrote of a new kind of faith, one that is not about God but about people. In his poem sequence, "I

---

1      Rabbi Kalonymous Kalman Shapira, Parashat Zakhor, 1942.
2      Rabbi Kalonymous Kalman Shapira, Parashat Hanukkah, 1941.

Wasn't One Of The Six Million: And What Is My Life Span? Open Closed Open" he wrote,

> "I believe with perfect faith that at this very moment
> millions of human beings are standing at crossroads,
> in jungles and deserts
> showing each other where to turn,
> what the right way is, which direction..."[3]

He imagines each of us at a crossroad, each of us lost perhaps in our own way. Yet "with excited voices, with a wave of the hand, a nod of our head," we still jump forward to help each other. This is his vision of "perfect faith."

I do not know what the future holds, but I want to live in Yehuda Amichai's Israel, one where we have perfect faith in each other, where we stand at the crossroads, eager to ensure each other's safe arrival. And I know we cannot arrive at this Israel without the insistence on hope and a commitment to faith.

---

3    Yehuda Amichai, *Open Closed Open*, translated by Chana Bloch and Chana Kronfeld (Harcourt, New York; 2000), from *"I wasn't one of the six million: and what is my life span? Open closed open."*

# Rachel Adelman

*Tears of Protest, Tears of Hope*

The events of October 7th that devastated Israel with over 220 hostages and 1,400 slaughtered (while still counting) has turned me into a well-spring of tears. I have two grown children and five grandchildren in Israel – all safe for now (thank God). Yet I feel deep anguish over the nine-month-old baby, Kfir, abducted with his three-year-old brother and mother, as if he were my own grandson. When I hear the parents or grandparents calling for the return of their children who were taken hostage by Hamas, perhaps sealed in underground cells, I resonate with my namesake, Rachel the matriarch: *"Wailing, bitter weeping for her children; she refuses to be comforted for her children who are gone"* (Jeremiah 31:15). Leaping up from her grave, she would not be consoled, crying for those taken into captivity by the Babylonians; her weeping demanded that they return (Rashi on Gen. 48:7; Eicha Rabbah, Petichta 24). Let my tears refuse comfort like hers, let them be tears of protest, tears of hope.

I imagine God weeping too. In the first redemption, just before the Exodus from Egypt, God appeared to Moses as fire in a bush that was not consumed (Exodus 3:2). The midrash asks: why a thorn-bush?

> *"I sleep, but my heart is awake. Listen! my lover is knocking. 'Open to me, my sister, my beloved, my dove, my perfect one [tamati]; for my head is wet with dew, my locks with the drops of the night'"* (Song of Songs 5:2)....R. Yannai said: just as twins [tomim] feel—when one has an aching head, the other feels his pain—so too God feels: "With him

(the nation), I will be in dire straits ['imo anokhi be-tzar]" (Psalm 91:51), and it says: "In all their dire straits, [God] is in dire straits [be-khol tzaratam, lo tzar]" (Isaiah 63:9). God said to them: If you (Moses) don't feel that I am steeped in suffering as Israel is steeped in suffering, then know from the place that I speak to you, from the thorns, I am a partner (so to speak) in their suffering. "An angel of the Lord appeared to him in a blazing fire from within the thorn-bush..." (Exod. 3:2). (Exodus Rabbah 2:2, ed. Shinan my translation).

To love Israel, the people and the land, is to feel the wakeful heart through sleep, over thousands of miles of separation, as the beloved in Song of Songs hears her lover call: "Open to me, my sister, my beloved, my dove, my perfect one [tamati]" (5:2). It is to feel radical empathy, to feel pain symbiotically as identical twins [te'umim] often feel the other's pain across distance.

In our time, God is not somewhere out there to redeem us from our pain. God is in the collective pulse of the Jewish people.

So I propose a creative re-reading of Isaiah's words about divine compassion, substituting God for Kelal Yisrael (the Jewish people as a whole). (After all, the subject of the pronoun 'he' or 'his' is never made explicit in the verse): "In all Israel's dire straits, we (the Jewish people) are in straits; no angel of the presence saves them; rather, in (our) love and in (our) pity (we) redeem them; lift them up and carry them as in the days of old" (Isaiah 63:9, following the ketiv).

So may we soon hear the prophet's words to Rachel resonate: "Restrain your voice from weeping, your eyes from shedding tears; For there is a reward for your labour... and a hope for your future....Your children shall return to their borders" (Jeremiah 31:16-17).

# Harris Bor
## *Sukkot: Gathering and Remaining*

This war has battered our sense of security, our faith in humanity, our hopes for a peaceful future. Our minds can't make sense of what has happened or imagine what will be. Our emotions too are overwhelmed as we grapple with anger, fear, guilt, feelings of isolation, and utter confusion. No answer fits, no feeling seems adequate. We are left with a void, created not only by those missing or lost, but the enormity of unknowing.

No wonder then that many of us are thrown back on faith, drawn to respond in the way we have so often responded, by seeking God even his concealment, while recognizing that there is no simple answer or second-guessing God's will. Tradition lends itself to such an exercise. I initially engaged by writing a poem based on a well-known medieval *kinah* (lament), but also take some inspiration from ideas associated with Sukkot and Shemini Azeret, when all this started.

The *sukkah* represents life's insecurity. The mystic, Rav Zadok Hakohen of Lublin (1824-1900) writes: "This is what the commandment [to sit in a] sukkah involves... We leave our fixed abode and enter a temporary abode because nothing for the Jew is ever secure. His lodging and home are in the air." Nothing feels more true.

Israel has been shaken to its core and faces unprecedented challenges as its people leave the security of their homes to fight. The diaspora is also under attack. We live suspended in air. Yet

Rav Zadok offers words of encouragement. We thrive in this state because we cleave to a divinity that also has no fixed abode, who resides *"entirely in air"* (*Machshavot Charutz*, 12). God then is found in the liminal, the very no-place we now reside. It's here that we discover our strength.

A further theme of Sukkot and Shemini Atzeret is *achdut* (unity or oneness). As so often in our history, when disaster strikes, we come together as one body with one heart. This is our power. The Sfat Emet (1847-1905), another mystic writing at the same time as Rav Zadok, explains that Sukkot is called the "Festival of Ingathering" because its purpose is to unify the people under the Sukkah's canopy, symbolic of the divine presence.

As for Shemini Atzeret, the word *atzeret* means "stopping" or "remaining." The Sfat Emet plays on this when he writes that "if the people enter the sukkah for the sake of heaven, they will remain in the state [of unity] even when they re-enter their homes" (*Devarim, Sukkot*, 30.1).

On Shemini Atzeret, after those terrible events, Israel put aside its differences and embraced unity. Maintaining such unity is a constant effort because it demands balancing competing outlooks and interests and fostering respect. But we now understand its importance, not only to our well-being but to our very survival, and must therefore work to maintain it in the weeks ahead and when the people return home. May that day come speedily and may all humanity dwell in peace and tranquillity.

# Alexander Goldberg
*Time Is on Our Side*

In the darkness, my room was illuminated by a text. It was from Bisan, a Palestinian friend who lives in Europe. Before I could fully read it, it disappeared; she had deleted it.

The abruptness of the message's disappearance captured my immediate attention. Worried, I replied, "How are you and your family?" Our ensuing exchanges were filled with mutual concerns for each other's families, about the sad news we both had encountered from many Jewish and Arab, Israeli and Palestinian friends. We gave ourselves brief reassurances that for now, both our families were unscathed and that one day everything would be better. Most importantly we agreed to pray for one another and for the wellbeing of our close relatives living in the region.

This small interaction, set against the Middle East's complexities, stirred introspection. I was compelled to reflect on timeless virtues: love, unity, and shared humanity, particularly in a landscape where hope is fleeting. Recent days have been tough and brought calls from friends grieving loved ones, anxious about known hostages or experiences of violence both there and closer to home. I ponder: if Abraham witnessed the division among Jews, Muslims, and Christians – his descendants – how would he react?

In his darkest days, the Torah says Abraham grieved for his loss but when the time was right 'rose up' to continue his work to create and build a future, our future.

In this moment, in navigating these turbulent times, I'm uplifted and comforted, by exchanges like that with Bisan and unexpected calls from Muslim and Christian leaders, checking in on me or simply wishing me "Shabbat Shalom," emphasising the profound power of human connection in dispelling darkness. The timeless teaching "Love your neighbour as yourself" has never felt more relevant and sadly tested than now. For me, it prompts us to recognise the Divine image in everyone. And reminds me true friendship doesn't require agreement on all matters, but simply genuine presence, understanding, love, and respect.

When it felt our efforts in intercommunal relations had stumbled into hopelessness, these small exchanges have rekindled hope, allowing myself to dream again. Without such dreams, we lack a crucial human virtue: the ability to imagine a brighter future together. The idea that faith could be a bridge rather than a barrier is a notion that perhaps seems almost utopian now, but its very possibility fuels the persistence of these shared dreams: that one day soon we will need a new Covenant between all the children of Abraham: based on hope, security, peace and understanding of all, by all, for all.

The Talmud advises, *"As long as the candle burns, one can correct."*

Time, though fleeting, is on our side. Every shared gesture or kind word fortifies our collective spirit to try better, to start rebuilding faith in the other. Like Noah and his family sitting in his ark after the world was destroyed, I too dream that the dove returns with the olive branch: an olive branch of peace between neighbours. Shalom, Salaam. Peace.

# Aviva Lauer
*Putting the* ר.ש.י *in* ישראל

On the saddest day of the Jewish year, the 9th of Av, which commemorates the ruinous destruction of both our Temples and so many other devastating annihilations throughout our history, we ask ourselves, God, and the universe: *Eicha?* How?

This is a stunned question, an angry question, a giving-up sort of question. Can it also be a figuring-out-our-way-back question? In the aftermath of Simchat Torah 5784 we are also asking, *Eicha?* over and over.

How could this have happened?
How could Hamas have done this?
How could the Israeli defence establishment have gotten so complacent and gotten things so wrong?
How could God have let this happen?
How can we go on?

When perhaps the earliest permutation of Hamas brutally attacked our people upon their exodus from Egypt, the Torah immediately answers some of these questions in the retelling of the episode in Deuteronomy (25:17-18):

*"Remember what Amalek did to you on your journey, after you left Egypt — how, undeterred by fear of God, he surprised you on the march, when you were famished and weary, and cut down all the stragglers in your rear."*

*How could this have happened?*
We were so weary from the generations of slavery. We were so tired from the roller coaster of the Exodus. We were so hungry and thirsty and needed time to overcome trauma and heartbreak and find our way again. We just needed a break. R. Samson Raphael Hirsch (19th century, Central Europe) notes that the nation was completely *"preoccupied with thoughts and worries that were as far as could be from war; this was a journey of a multitude of homeless people walking through the desert."* Of course they weren't expecting something like this to happen! And we couldn't have expected them to foresee it.

*How could they have done this to us?*
They were not God-fearing people, the Amalekites. R. Dovid Zvi Hoffman (also 19th century, Central Europe) explains that even normal idol worshippers' etiquette would dictate refraining from attacking a group of people minding their own business peacefully, just passing through - and how much more so from falling upon the weak and young and harmless and trusting. But Amalek didn't abide by normal rules. They couldn't have cared less about what others would think or what God would think or what normal human mores dictate.

I will leave the disbelief over the defence establishment's disastrous sense of security to the analysts and the heartbreaking investigation of God's care to the theologians. But I will attempt a thought as to our last 'how' question:

*How can and will we go on from here?*
Rav Hirsch discusses why the story of Amalek is repeated here in Deuteronomy, and why specifically in this context, especially after

having been told in 'real time' back in Exodus 17. The context here, he says, is a wide-ranging 'ideal sketch' of how the Jewish people are meant to function and flourish in society, among themselves and with others. Our "national character must be one of goodwill, consideration, generosity and kindness towards every living thing, as is emphasised over and over in the final chapters of God's Torah. We find that people must be prepared at all times to do good, and must be unable due to the core of their nature to do bad to anyone else." That is what makes us Israel - decent and honourable - and what puts the ר.ש.י in ישראל.

The character of Amalek is brought to bear in this context as the utter antithesis of who we are and how we are meant to be. They are ruthless, they are brutal, they are callous, they are sadistic. They are everything we must never let ourselves be, and the juxtaposition here indicates this pointedly.

This gives me relief and gives me hope. Even, or especially, in the face of barbarism and inhumanity, we can continue on as our true selves. We don't have to harden ourselves. We needn't inure ourselves to helping others, to being vulnerable and caring. We should remain shocked at awful behaviour, and not expect it. We must, of course, watch out for ourselves. But we mustn't and don't have to let this change us.

This is not naïveté.
This is our charge.
This is who we are.
We can, therefore, go on.

# Joy Ladin
## *What All Schoolchildren Learn*

As atrocity begets atrocity in Israel and Gaza, I keep remembering what W.H. Auden wrote in "September 1, 1939," as the Holocaust loomed:

> *I and the public know*
> *What all schoolchildren learn,*
> *Those to whom evil is done*
> *Do evil in return.*

Evil has been done to us, in the form of 1400 murders, hundreds of captives, homes and lives demolished. Evil is being done to us, in the rain of rockets and continued violence.

For many Jews, Hamas's murderous rampage traumatically recalls the Holocaust and pogroms that preceded it. We couldn't stop the perpetrators then, so we must do anything and everything to stop them now, wiping out everyone who does or might try to be evil to us.

But Auden, and every Israeli, knows what to expect in return.

And Auden's rhyme reminds us that no matter how much emotional sense such reactions to Hamas's violence may make, there is no moral difference between evil that is done to us and evil we do in return.

The Nakba and occupation don't make Hamas's assault on civilians less or other than evil, and neither Hamas nor the Holocaust make Israel's decades of military rule over Palestinian civilians or the bombardment of apartment buildings and refugee camps and cutting off of food, water, and electricity to the people trapped in Gaza less or other than evil. No terrorism or oppression makes killing children and the elderly, whether by beheading or bombing, siege or "surgical strikes," less evil.

When we do evil we do evil, no matter what evil we have suffered.

And after so many decades of violence, we don't need Auden to teach us that doing evil to those who have done evil to us doesn't make us safe. The evil we do, however necessary or justified or emotionally urgent it feels, will inspire those we bereave and injure, dehydrate and starve, to return evil for evil. Injustice begets injustice; bombing civilians begets bombing civilians; massacre begets massacre.

We can't kill our way to security or *shalom*.

Horrific as Hamas's atrocities are, they don't mark the beginning of another Holocaust. Despite all the murders, Israel and the Jewish people will survive. Israel's military might ensures that whatever evil Hamas does, Israel will be able to do far more in return – in recent Gaza conflicts, about 10 Palestinians have been killed for every Israeli death.

Those to whom evil is done will do evil in return.

That's what schoolchildren learn. But adults can separate our traumatic past from our militarily dominant present; we can recognise the evil that has been done to us as a moment in Auden's tragic cycle, a cycle we perpetuate by devastating the people of Gaza and continuing the occupation.

We can break the cycle by refusing to return evil for evil, and dedicating ourselves to the hard and dangerous work of doing justice, loving mercy, and making true *shalom* for all who call the Land their home.

# Jonathan Romain

*First Loves*

We always remember the person with whom we first fell in love.

It is the same with our relationship with Israel. The Israel of our youth is the one that most colours our attitude now.

This is not to say we cannot alter our views over the years, but our default emotional position is largely pre-set.

For my parents' generation, who witnessed the birth of Israel, it was a miracle they never expected. The child born out of the ashes of the Holocaust that was both brave and vulnerable. In their mind's eye, despite the changes that occurred, Israelis were always the *kibbutznik* in his/her shorts and *kova*.

My generation's first awareness of Israel was the 1967 War. The time when everyone wore SuperGolda T-shirts and Moshe Dayan's eyepatch was instantly recognisable. Not only were Israelis heroes, but we Jews walked tall. Our self-image changed overnight from victims to warriors.

For my children, they grew up after 1982 with images of the massacres in the refugee camps of Sabra and Shatilla. It may have been Lebanese militias that did the killing, but Israel's image was tarnished, while the terms "Israeli occupation" and "Palestinian rights" constantly rang out.

Obviously the above is a generalisation, but it does highlight a generational divide in the approach of British Jews towards Israel, with views ranging widely from "Israel - right or wrong" to "Not in my name".

They also explain why Israel has changed from being a unifying factor for British Jews to a divisive one. There was a time, for instance, when Orthodox and Progressive rabbis never met in public, but they did come together for Israel events.

Now, however, Israel and how it deals with the Palestinian issue is a much more polarising factor than the religious gap.

These different starting points also affect which side of the fence we come down on in the terrible dilemma facing Israel today. We all recognise that what Hamas did on 7th October was appalling and abhorrently different from any of the previous conflicts between Israel and her opponent.

But here the agreement ends. For some, this means Israel has to eradicate Hamas whatever the cost to the Palestinian civilians who are caught up in the crossfire. If they are killed, it is the fault of Hamas for deliberately embedding itself amongst schools, hospitals and residential areas.

For others, Israel cannot fight evil with evil. The loss of so many Israelis cannot justify the equal number of Palestinian deaths, and certainly not a far greater number of them. They are victims of Hamas too. As Abraham challenged God over the proposed destruction of Sodom and Gomorrah, many ask today: "Will you sweep away the innocent with the wicked too?" (Gen. 18.23).

But while disagreeing over policies, one common thread holds true: we support the people of Israel and hold the land of Israel precious.

Conversely, the thought of Israel not existing is a scenario all three generations would find unacceptable. The fight for peace and co-existence remains the dream we strive to make true.

# Shimon Felix

*Living with the Dissonance*

The basic ethical issue which lies at the centre of Israel's war against Hamas is the attempt to balance the obvious need to destroy the terrorist group - Israel will not be safe from the kind of atrocities committed by Hamas on Simhat Torah until they are eliminated - with the equally obvious need to not harm innocent civilians while doing so. One of the war crimes committed by Hamas, the taking of hostages, including infants and old people, further complicates the equation: while fighting Hamas, can we also protect our own people? And, of course, we also fear for the lives of our soldiers, another emotional, and tactical, consideration.

The Israeli government and the public have, by and large, decided that there is no possibility of eliminating the threat of Hamas through non-military means, an assessment which I believe recent history has proven to be correct. There is strong public opinion in favour of prosecuting the war in spite of the strong possibility that there will be civilian casualties. The Israeli people also desperately want the hostages to be safely freed, but are not sure if our attack on Gaza will harm or help. Nonetheless, there is broad support for the military campaign.

Around the world, there are many taking different positions, ranging from a legitimate concern for the lives of Gazan civilians, as well as an equally legitimate concern for the future of both Israelis and Palestinians, to outright antisemites, who grotesquely rejoice in the slaughter of Israelis and the possible erasure of the Jewish State.

I am supportive of the war, and feel strongly that Israel will be a severely crippled country if we do not rid ourselves of the existential threats that have been allowed to grow to monstrous proportions on our borders. I am, however, profoundly troubled by the loss of life that the war will cause, among both Palestinians and Israeli hostages and soldiers. As a result, I sometimes find myself wondering if we perhaps should find another way to solve the problem of Hamas - and Hezbollah - a more peaceful, less deadly, way. I am often caught in a kind of mental and emotional loop - positive that we must destroy these butchers, while extremely troubled by the cost, on both sides.

I think our tradition wants us to live in this dissonance. Here are two stories from the Torah:

After Avraham successfully fought a war to free his nephew Lot, who had been taken hostage, the commentator Rashi tells us that Avraham was afraid that he had used up all his credit with God, when He came to his aid and assisted him in killing his enemies. God informs him that he has more than just used up his credit: on some level, Avraham deserves to be punished for all the people he killed. But, God reassures him, He will protect him from being punished for that.

When the patriarch Yaakov was about to confront his brother, Esav, from whom, years earlier, after tricking him out of his birthright and blessings, he had fled for his life, we are told that *"Yaakov was very afraid, and saddened."* The Rabbis explain that he was afraid of being killed, and saddened by the possibility that he may be forced to kill.

The complicated emotions in both stories, the fear of being killed and the great distaste for killing, the understanding of the wrongness of war, while at the same time being willing to do battle if we must, are what we, in Israel, are feeling now. It is right that we are saddened and burdened by the possibility of killing, and good that we are fearful for Jewish lives.

It is also right that we, in spite of these concerns, are going into battle. Holding these conflicting positions in our hearts and minds is the Jewish imperative. It guides us as we attempt to rid ourselves, and the world, of the unspeakable evil of anti-Israel lies, butchery, and terror. May God be with us, may we not use up all our credit with Him, and may we continue to be troubled by the moral dilemmas with which war presents us.

# Samuel Lebens
*The Call to Action*

I want to share something that I've learnt from Israeli society in these troubled times, which has given me a new insight into a central Biblical puzzle.

Since the evening of the 7th of October, as Simchat Torah departed, I have found it almost impossible, except on Shabbat, to prise myself away from my phone, wanting to consume as much news about the war as I can. But to be so dependent on the news, and to be so absorbed in the conflict all day long, precipitates depression and a spiral of despair. The only thing I have found that can compete with the news, is the spirit of volunteerism that has swept the country.

So many Israelis are busying themselves with initiatives to supply our soldiers with food, and life-saving equipment. Others are making sure that the many displaced citizens of Israel have clothes, and that their children should have toys to play with, and activities to structure their days. Some have taken it upon themselves to attend funerals and shiva houses of people they don't yet know. The people of Israel, after months of bitter division, have united like at no time that I can remember, in my 40 years of life.

In the Bible, the first sin committed by humanity is the consumption of the forbidden fruit; the fruit of the tree of knowledge of good and bad. It has been asked why it should be sinful to eat from the tree of knowledge. Isn't knowledge always a good thing? Can it be that Adam and Eve became more perfect, because more knowledgeable, as a result of their sin? This question receives a two-chapter long response from Maimonides in his *Guide to the Perplexed*. But Israeli society has taught me a different answer.

The answer is this - knowledge isn't always a good thing. About some things, you can know too much. Or, you can know too much detail. I didn't need to see all of the photographs or the videos, to know the gruesome reality. I didn't need to read the umpteenth opinion piece to know the contours of the situation. The Midrash suggests that Adam and Eve were going to be permitted to eat of that tree, but only when the time was right, only when it was appropriate to do so. It turns out that there is something much better for your mental health than filling yourself up with the knowledge of good and evil, and that is simply doing the good! And in this time of darkness, that is what Israeli civil society has committed itself to doing.

The lesson isn't to neglect knowledge and the life of the mind. But the idea is to become sensitive to the sort of knowledge we need to accumulate, and to know what sorts of knowledge, and what level of detail, might actually be harmful to us. The idea, moreover, is to be sensitive to the call to action, even as you're drawn to the constant stream of news. In the words of the Mishna (Avot 1:17), "Study isn't of primary importance, [because] action is [even more important]."

# Carl S. Ehrlich
## *Memory and Marginalisation*

As scholars such as Yosef Hayim Yerushalmi have pointed out, the Jews are a people of memory. All our celebrations are in memory of events in our people's history (or historical memory), even those that commemorate creation, which is the supposed moment in time with which our story and that of all humanity begins.

But we aren't the only people with a memory. The horrific massacre of October 7, 2023, was deliberately chosen to take place on a Jewish holiday almost exactly fifty years after the surprise attack on Yom Kippur 1973, which almost led to the destruction of the Jewish State. There is no doubt that this was intended to send a brutal message to Israel and its supporters.

Perspicacious pundits immediately predicted that the world would mourn the slaughtered Jews for a day or two but would then forget about them and revert to the default position of castigating Israel for responding to the unspeakable horrors of that day and defending itself. And indeed, within a day or two, before the corpses of the innocent were cold, massive demonstrations began taking place throughout the world celebrating the deaths of Jews and pre-emptively attempting to hamper Israel's justified and justifiable response to the unimaginable atrocity of October 7th.

While the Allied forces in World War II understood that the only way to defeat nihilistic death-cults is to obliterate them so that something new and responsible could flower from their ruin, a policy that resulted in both post-Nazi Germany and post-Imperial

Japan rejoining the family of nations, the rules of the game have always been different for Israel. Time and again, world opinion and outside political pressure have conspired to constrain Israel from meeting its military and security goals. However, the resolve of Israel and the global Jewish community to finish the task appears stronger this time. Perhaps, this time Israel will be able to resist the external pressures to cease its campaign against Hamas and to rid its proximate neighbourhood of this scourge.

The lack of support for Israel at this moment in time, particularly among western academics and their students, is both worrisome and upsetting, and does not augur well for the future. Many actively support Hamas and find justification for its despicable actions. Modern critical theories – such as that of intersectionality – allow no room for Jews as victim rather than oppressor, in this manner, deny the Jewish experience both contemporary and historical. Jewish professors and their students feel abandoned and marginalised.

Anti-Israel and anti-Jewish sentiment in academia is nothing new. I remember it well from my own undergraduate days half a century ago. Indeed, I recall reading an article by Cynthia Ozick one year after the Yom Kippur War that was entitled "All the World Wants the Jews Dead." At the time, I found the title overly provocative, but I quickly learned how true it is. And unfortunately, it appears more trenchant with each passing year. Hence, when I saw the title of Dara Horn's recent *People Love Dead Jews: Reports from a Haunted Present*, my reaction was one of world-weary assent. The more things change, the more they stay the same.

Nevertheless, I am able to find some hope and succour in texts such as Isaiah 63, in which an anonymous prophet of the post-exilic period, whose words have been tacked onto the prophecies attributed to the eponymous eighth-century BCE Isaiah, envisions God as a warrior returning from battle:

וְאַבִּיט וְאֵין עֹזֵר וְאֶשְׁתּוֹמֵם וְאֵין סוֹמֵךְ וַתּוֹשַׁע־לִי זְרֹעִי וַחֲמָתִי הִיא סְמָכָתְנִי:

*I looked around, but there was no one to help (me);*
*I was astonished that there was no one to support (me).*
*Therefore, my own arm saved me,*
*and my burning anger supported me. (Isa 63:5)*

This text tells me...tells us...that our fate is in our own hands. Even if we are abandoned by the world, if we rely on our own might and strength, and on the justice of our cause, we will prevail. We have no other choice if we wish to survive.

# Jeremy Gordon
*Hope in A Broken World*

Emil Fackenheim's masterwork, *To Mend the World* starts with hopelessness. Surely, the great post-Holocaust writer suggests, the awfulness of the Holocaust renders all theorising about "good" and "evil" inauthentic. But Fackenheim refuses to yield to despair.

He finds something truly precious in the rubble of European Jewry: the very building blocks of a response.

> *"It is at [the point of Auschwitz] that our going-to-school-with-life...begins in earnest...And only in [the] context of [engaging with destruction] can the 'central question' of our whole inquiry be both asked and answered."*

The answer – hope - arises even in the depths of horror, for even there, in Auschwitz itself, there were acts of goodness. Even there, humanity found ways to insist on its possibility.

This approach is also at the heart of Melissa Raphael's brilliant book, *The Female Face of God in Auschwitz*. From survivor testimony, Raphael excavates countless tales of tiny acts of decency, even in the midst of tragedy. For Raphael these acts define something godly.

> *God could hardly find her way through the darkness—but the darkness was not her disappearance. However momentarily, the*

*spark generated between the seeing and seen face was analogous to a Sabbath candle inviting God's presence—Shekhinah—into Auschwitz. Even the most infinitesimal spark of light was enough to illuminate— if only momentarily—the grey face of the other and so refract God into the toppling world.*

And so to Israel. In the bleak aftermath of atrocities that have evoked, in the waking nightmare of lovers of Israel, memories of the Holocaust, it would be possible to yield to despair. But yet, but yet. Just last night, as I type, 700 Jews and Arabs attended a Solidarity Rally in Haifa. Tomorrow, as I type, Magen Inon, whose mother and father were both murdered by Hamas terrorists, will speak at a rally. He has written;

*From this unbearable feeling of pain and distress, I wish to speak about what I believe is my parents' legacy. People from both sides of the border have good reasons to hate one another. But this cannot be the only option. My family does not seek revenge... Our shared future is based on the belief that all human beings are equal, and deserving of respect and safety. This is how I was raised and how I am raising my own children. In the long term, and even if it's very far away, the only real future is that of hope and peace.*

Across Israel, civil society thrives, with new purpose as acts of love, support and kindness prop up the lives of those left orphaned, wounded and bereft. There is an Israel emerging from this horror that still has the power to love, that still has hope and that still has the power, as Fackenheim termed it, *To Mend the World.*

Even now, even after this. I still believe.

# Contributors

**Rachel Adelman** is Associate Professor of Hebrew Bible at Boston's Hebrew College. She holds a Ph.D. in Hebrew Literature from the Hebrew University of Jerusalem and is the author of *The Return of the Repressed: Pirqe de-Rabbi Eliezer and the Pseudepigrapha* and *The Female Ruse: Women's Deception and Divine Sanction in the Hebrew Bible*.

**Chaya Baker** was ordained in 2007 by the Schechter Rabbinical Seminary. She has served, since her ordination, as the rabbi of Kehillat Ramot-Zion in French Hill, Jerusalem. For the past eight years, she has served as Coordinator of Practical Rabbinics at SRS. In 2015 she was the first Masorti rabbi – and the first ever female rabbi – to be invited to teach Torah at the Israeli President's residence.

**Harris Bor** is a Fellow and Lecturer at the London School of Jewish Studies and a barrister (trial advocate) specialising in international arbitration and commercial litigation. He holds a PhD in Theology from the University of Cambridge. He obtained rabbinic ordination from the Montefiore Endowment, and has been a visiting scholar at Harvard University and University College London.

**Nathan Lopes Cardozo** is the Founder and Dean of the David Cardozo Academy and the Bet Midrash of Avraham Avinu in Jerusalem. He is the author of 13 books and numerous articles in both English and Hebrew. He heads a think tank focussed on finding new halachic and philosophical approaches to religious issues facing the Jewish People and the State of Israel.

**Eliezer Diamond** is the Rabbi Judah Nadich Associate Professor of Talmud and Rabbinics at The Jewish Theological Seminary. He teaches courses in rabbinic literature and introductory, intermediate, and advanced Talmud studies.

**Carl S. Ehrlich** is University Professor of History and Humanities, and former Director of the Israel and Golda Koschitzky Centre for Jewish Studies, at York University (Canada). Among his areas of interest are synchronic, diachronic, and contextual approaches to the biblical text and Israelite civilization. His recent publications include the (co-)edited collections *From an Antique Land: An Introduction to Ancient Near Eastern Literature* (2009), *Israel and the Diaspora: Jewish Connectivity in a Changing World* (2022), and *Jewish Studies on Premodern Periods: A Handbook* (2023).

**Miriam Feldman-Kaye** is a Lecturer in Jewish Philosophy at Bar-Ilan University and Associate Visiting Lecturer at the Jewish Theological Seminary. Miriam is Editor of the international *St Andrews University Encyclopaedia of Jewish Theology*. She previously co-founded and directed the Faith and Belief Forum Middle East, a dialogue project in Israel dedicated to developing relations between faith communities in partnership with the Hebrew University and the Truman Research Institute for the Development of Peace and Reconciliation. Her publications include her book *Jewish Theology for a Postmodern Age* (LUP & Littman).

**Shimon Felix** is the Executive Director Emeritus of the program at the Bronfman Fellowship. He received his rabbinic ordination from Yeshivat Hamivtar, where he served as educational director. Rabbi Felix has worked in a wide variety of educational programs including Michelelet Bruria, the Israeli school system and Yakar.

**Miri Fenton** is writing her PhD in Mediaeval History, comparing and contrasting Jewish community life in the Crown of Aragon and Ashkenaz, 1100-1347. Miri holds a BA in history, and an MPhil in Philosophy of Religion, from the University of Cambridge. She has been working with *October7.org*, an online archive of personal testimonies from the Hamas attacks on Simchat Torah.

**Reuven Firestone** is an American academic and historian of religion, who serves as the Regenstein Professor in Medieval Judaism and Islam at the Hebrew Union College - Jewish Institute of Religion's Skirball Campus in Los Angeles and Affiliate Professor of Religion at the University of Southern California. He has researched and written extensively on the topics of religious violence and holy war in Islam and Judaism.

**David Frankel** is Associate Professor of Bible at the Schechter Institute of Jewish Studies. He has been on the faculty since 1992. He earned his PhD from the Hebrew University of Jerusalem. His publications include *The Murmuring Stories of the Priestly School* and *The Land of Canaan and the Destiny of Israel.*

**Naomi Graetz** taught English at Ben Gurion University of the Negev for 35 years. She is the author of *Unlocking the Garden: A Feminist Jewish Look at the Bible, Midrash and God* (Gorgias Press), *The Rabbi's Wife Plays at Murder* (Shiluv Press), *S/He Created Them: Feminist Retellings of Biblical Stories* (Gorgias Press,), and *Silence is Deadly: Judaism Confronts Wifebeating* (Jason Aronson).

**Alexander Goldberg** is the Dean of Religious Life and Belief, Coordinating and the Jewish Chaplain to the University of Surrey, England, a rabbi, barrister, and human rights activist. He is one of the regular contributors to BBC Radio 2's Pause for Thought.

**David Golinkin** is President of The Schechter Institutes, Inc. and President Emeritus of the Schechter Institute of Jewish Studies. For twenty years he served as Chair of the *Va'ad Halakhah* (Law Committee) of the Rabbinical Assembly which gives halakhic guidance to the Masorti Movement in Israel. He is the founder and director of the Institute of Applied Halakhah at Schechter and also directs the Center for Women in Jewish Law.

**Jeremy Gordon** is the rabbi of New London Synagogue. He has a first class honours degree in Law from Cambridge University and subsequently went to work in television. His love of Judaism was really ignited at the Limmud Conference in December 1995. This marked the start of a decade of study in England, at the Hebrew University and the Conservative Yeshiva in Jerusalem and the Jewish Theological Seminary in New York. He graduated from JTS with Rabbinic Ordination, a Masters in Midrash (Rabbinic Exegesis) and a number of academic awards.

**Art Green** is an American scholar of Jewish mysticism and Neo-Hasidic theologian. He was a founding dean of the non-denominational rabbinical program at Hebrew College in Boston. He has published both academic works on the intellectual history of Jewish mysticism and Hasidism, as well as writings of a more personal theological sort.

**Mark Greenspan** is the emeritus spiritual leader of the Oceanside Jewish Center. He is a graduate of the Joint Program of the Jewish Theological Seminary and Columbia University. He has been a congregational rabbi for almost forty years, serving synagogues in New York, Tennessee and Pennsylvania. He has translated nineteen commentaries on the Haggadah over the past two decades.

**Herzl Hefter** is the founder and Rosh Beit Midrash Har'el in memory of Belda Kaufman Lindenbaum, in Jerusalem. He has written numerous articles related to modernity and Hasidic thought.

**Menachem Kellner** is an American-Israeli academic and scholar of mediaeval Jewish philosophy with a particular focus on Maimonides. He is a retired Professor of Jewish Thought at the University of Haifa and is the founding chair of the Department of Philosophy and Jewish Thought at Shalem College in Jerusalem. His book *Must A Jew Believe Anything?* was a Koret Jewish Book Award finalist.

**David-Seth Kirshner** is the Rabbi of Temple Emanu-El, in Closter, New Jersey. He has written articles and been featured in many media sources and is regularly published in the Jewish Standard, The Times of Israel and The New York Times.

**Joy Ladin** is an American poet and the former David and Ruth Gottesman Chair in English at Stern College for Women at Yeshiva University. She was the first openly transgender professor at an Orthodox Jewish institution. She has written numerous books of poetry including *The Book of Anna*, which was a National Jewish Book Award winner.

**Aviva Lauer** is the Director of the Pardes Center for Jewish Educators. She majored in Jewish Studies at Yeshiva University's Stern College for Women, and earned a Masters degree in Midrash at the Schechter Institute of Jewish Studies. She is a Jewish educator with 25 years of experience in curriculum development, classroom teaching, school administration and educational consulting.

**Samuel Lebens** is associate Professor in the philosophy department at the University of Haifa. He is also an Orthodox Rabbi and Jewish educator. He is the author of several books including *A Guide For The Jewish Undecided* and most recently *Thinking about Stories: An Introduction to Philosophy of Fiction*, which he co-authored with Tatjana von Solodkoff.

**Jane Liddell-King** is a poet. Her prize-winning work has been published in Britain, Germany, and the United States. She has given readings of her work at numerous events. Previously, she collaborated with artist Nancy Tingey on an exhibition entitled, The Golden Calf which was shown in both Britain and Australia. She is the author of three plays and many articles and reviews.

**Dalia Marx** is the Rabbi Aaron D. Panken Professor of Liturgy and Midrash at HUC-JIR's Taube Family Campus in Jerusalem, and teaches in various academic institutions in Israel and Europe. Marx, a tenth generation Jerusalemite, earned her doctorate at the Hebrew University and her rabbinic ordination at HUC-JIR. She is the lead editor of the Israeli Reform siddur, *Tfillat HaAdam*. Her book From *Time to Time: Journeys in the Jewish Calendar* was translated into several languages.

**Paul Mendes-Flohr** is Professor Emeritus of Jewish Thought at the Hebrew University of Jerusalem. He is co-author and co-editor, with Joshua Reinharz, of a book for modern Jewish history *The Jew in the*

*Modern World: A Documentary History* and with Arthur Cohen of a book on contemporary Jewish religious thought. In 2019 he published a highly regarded biography of Martin Buber entitled *Martin Buber: A Life of Faith and Dissent.* He recently began work on The Global Lehrhaus, an international platform for education and reflection on issues of common concern.

**Francis Nataf** is a Jerusalem-based thinker, writer, and educator. He is the author of the *Redeeming Relevance in the Torah* series and of many articles on religious thought, biblical studies, and current events and is Associate Editor of the Jewish Bible Quarterly.

**David Newman OBE** is a British-Israeli scholar in political geography and geopolitics. He is a professor at the Ben-Gurion University of the Negev Department of Politics and Government and was this department's first chairperson. He also served as chief editor of the academic journal Geopolitics and as Dean of BGU's Faculty of Humanities and Social Sciences.

**Ben Rebuck** hosts the podcast entitled Campaign Against Antisemitism. He is a Jewish vegan chef and activist who runs the popular Instagram page Ben's Vegan Kitchen (@bensvegankitchen).

**Jonathan Romain** is a writer and broadcaster and director of Maidenhead Synagogue, in Berkshire, England. He has a Ph.D. in the history of British Jewry. He writes for a number of national newspapers and appears regularly on radio and television.

**David Mevorach Seidenberg** received his doctoral degree from the Jewish Theological Seminary for his work on ecology and Kabbalah and was ordained by both the Jewish Theological Seminary and Rabbi

Zalman Schachter-Shalomi. He teaches Jewish thought in Europe, Israel and throughout North America, in communities and universities, and through his organisation, *neohasid.org*.

**Avi Solomon** is an independent researcher engaged in translating the works of Abraham Abulafia from Hebrew into English for the benefit of a wider reading public.

**Marc Soloway** has been the Rabbi of Bonai Shalom in Colorado, USA since 2004, the same year that he was ordained at The Ziegler School for Rabbinic Studies at The American Jewish University in Los Angeles. Marc is a fellow of Rabbis without Borders and was in the Forward's 2014 list of America's most influential rabbis.

**Avi Strausberg** is the Senior Director of National Learning Initiatives at Hadar, and is based in Washington, DC. Previously, Rabbi Strausberg served as the Director of Congregational Learning of Temple of Aaron in St. Paul, Minnesota. She received her rabbinic ordination from Hebrew College in Boston and is a Wexner Graduate Fellow. She also holds a Masters in Jewish Education.

**Tzemah Yoreh** is the rabbi of The City Congregation in New York and one of the intellectual leaders of Jewish humanism. He attended the Hebrew University of Jerusalem, where he obtained his Ph.D. in biblical criticism in record time. He earned a second Ph.D. in Ancient Wisdom Literature at the University of Toronto.

**Daniel Zucker** is the Associate Rabbi at White Meadow Temple/ Or Hadash in Rockaway, and President and CEO of Americans for Democracy in the Middle-East. He holds an M.A. in Hebrew Letters, a Doctor of Divinity from JTS, and rabbinic ordination from HUC-JIR.

# Editors

**Adam Zagoria-Moffet** is the rabbi of St.
Albans Masorti Synagogue in Hertfordshire,
the Director of the Louis Jacobs Foundation,
and the Editor-in-Chief of Izzun Books. He
received ordination from the Jewish Theological
Seminary of America, where he also completed
a Masters in Jewish Thought.

**Simon Eder** is Education Director of the
Louis Jacobs Foundation. He hosts the podcast
Between the Lines in which he interviews
leading scholars on the weekly Torah portion,
drawing audiences from around the world. His
book, *Jewish Angle of the Week*, was a compilation
of his blog posts during Covid lockdown. He is
one of the founders of the Jewish community
in Dubai. He graduated from the University
of Cambridge with a degree in Theology and
Religious Studies.

Printed in Great Britain
by Amazon

31866486R00076